Improvising Adulthood

what I wish someone had told me

Amanda Hirsch

For more information, email hello@amandahirsch.com.

ISBN: 979-8-89316-405-3 - eBook
ISBN: 979-8-89316-406-0 - Paperback

Free Gift

Get inspired by stories from change makers and creative souls who are improvising adulthood, with bonus advice and lessons learned. Claim your free gift at amandahirsch.com/improv with special code READERBONUS.

For young people who crave meaningful and fulfilling lives, and for anyone who struggles to conform to other people's scripts

CONTENTS

"There is a vitality, a life force, an energy, a quickening that is translated through you into action, and because there is only one of you in all of time, this expression is unique. And if you block it, it will never exist through any other medium and it will be lost. The world will not have it."

- Choreographer Martha Graham

"I just want my stories to be mine."

- Author Lidia Yukanavich

FOREWORD

"That's what we're all doing, all the time, whether we know it or not. Whether we like it or not. Creating something on the spur of the moment with the materials at hand. We might just as well let the rest of it go..."

- Actor Alan Arkin in *An Improvised Life: A Memoir*

"Just suck it up."

I heard this a lot in my 20s, albeit not in so many words, both from other people and in my own head. I was riddled with angst. I quit multiple jobs. I was deeply unsatisfied with the script I thought I was supposed to follow: You get a job, you do the job, you pay your bills. It doesn't matter if it feels meaningful, it doesn't matter if you feel fulfilled — *it's just what you do.*

But I couldn't help it; I always craved more. I made choices that other people struggled to understand. Which made me feel like something was very, very wrong with me.

I don't feel that way anymore.

Now that I'm in my 40s, I feel a deep appreciation for how all the choices I've made have created a unique and fulfilling existence. I have strangers reaching out to me on LinkedIn to say, "I so admire your purpose-driven life." I'm the same person. It's just that now, people can see how all those "weird" choices I was making knit together to create a compelling whole. It's not like I set out to achieve any kind of master plan; I simply couldn't tolerate doing things "just because," so I made choices, and over the decades, those choices became a life.

I improvised, which is all that any of us can do: We make choices, without the benefit of seeing how the story ends. And then we look back and try to make sense of the story. And then, we keep making choices. There's no script. There's no outline. There's only us, and our willingness to choose.

If you take one thing away from this book, I hope it's this: *No one else can choose your life for you.* Only you know what's right for you, which isn't to say you can't learn from other people, only that they can't choose your happiness or fulfillment. That's your job, your responsibility as well as your privilege. And the best way to navigate that job is to give yourself over to the art of improvisation, one choice at a time.

HOW TO READ THIS BOOK

In the coming pages, I'll share the story of the choices I've made so far, in the hope that you might read something that helps you feel less alone and more confident as you make your own. We'll use improv as the way into recognizing and dealing with situations we encounter in our journey to figure out who we are and our place in this world. Regardless of your relationship to being on stage, the art of improvising adulthood does not require any literal, onstage performance of any sort; instead, it involves applying the skills that the best improvisors use to make something out of nothing, together, on the fly. Most of all, improvising adulthood means seeing your life as a creative act — specifically, an improv show, one you shape with every choice you make.

Here's how I've organized the book to help you navigate your journey.

- **Scenes:** Instead of chapters, I've organized the book into scenes, for funsies and to underscore that we are using the art of improv as a way of approaching life. Each scene's title reveals its thematic focus.

- **Make-believe improv theater:** Each scene opens with a fictional vignette set in and around a make-believe improv theater. I wanted to more vividly evoke the art form that provides the book's central metaphor, giving those of you who've never seen an improv show a better sense of what it's like.

- **My story:** Next I share personal stories relevant to the scene's focus, illustrating how I've improvised my own adulthood and distilling lessons I've learned along the way. My hope is that you'll see yourself in parts of my journey and that this will help you feel less alone. I also hope that looking at my life through the lens of improv will help you see how to apply this lens to your own life.

- **Prompts for reflection:** At the end of each scene, I share prompts for reflection, designed to help you apply what you've read to your own life. In an improv show, the performers often kick things off by getting a word of inspiration from the audience; think of the prompts as your word of inspiration and see where they take you. Maybe they'll help you think about an area of your life or a decision you're facing in a new way or bring more of a sense of spaciousness to your decision-making process.

SOME THINGS TO KNOW ABOUT THE AUTHOR, AKA ME

Here are some things you might want to know about me as you begin reading:

- I founded and run my own business, Mighty Forces, to help change makers and creative souls explore and share their voices and stories in authentic and compelling ways online. I've been working for myself for almost two decades, ever since leaving my role as editorial director of PBS.org, where I helped documentary filmmakers translate their stories to the web.

- I've given talks about the power of telling your story online everywhere from Harvard's Kennedy School and the National Press Club to coworking spaces and start-ups.

- My clients are deep, smart people who are committed to doing work that improves other people's lives. They work for organizations you've likely heard of, like Malala Fund, Melinda French Gates' Pivotal Ventures, Girl Scouts USA, TEDWomen, and Adobe. Others work for themselves, as entrepreneurs and artists.

- I have a background in improv comedy and have performed at festivals around the country. I've also given talks on applying improv's lessons to life at venues like Etsy and SXSW, often with my husband, Jordan; at SXSW, we were voted audience favorites. The principles of improv have become a fundamental basis of the way I live my life — much more on this in the pages ahead.

- I've written two books (counting this one!), and am an aspiring TV writer; one of my original scripts, "Yes, Andrea," was a finalist in the Sundance Episodic Lab.

- I'm a Taurus, an INFJ, and am famous for my early bedtimes, to the point that when my friends Katie and Zach make it an early night, they call it "Hirsching out."

- I live with Jordan, our daughter Ali, and our dog Clover in New York's Hudson Valley.

If you had sat me down at age 18 and asked, "Amanda, what will your adult life look like?", the only part of the above list that I could have predicted was the being-married-to-Jordan part, since we fell in love at the end of my senior year of high school. I might have had hope (but not a shred of confidence) that acting and writing would be in the mix. I would have probably said, "I'll have a master's degree in something"; unless the MFA program I quit halfway through counts (it does not), then, no master's degree for me, but then again, Jordan and I won on "Cash Cab" (true story), and I never saw *that* coming.

ONCE UPON A TIME, I DISCOVERED IMPROV

For me, the beginning of realizing improv was the gateway to living a life I loved happened shortly after the turn of the century. Back then, we hiked barefoot in the snow both ways to rent these things called "videotapes" from a place called "Blockbuster."

But for real: I was in my mid-20s, and I was standing on stage pretending to be a number two pencil. And I was blissed. Out.

I'd never thought of myself as a funny person, so when Jordan started taking improv classes, and encouraged me to join him, I was approximately zero percent interested. "It's not about being funny," he told me, over and over; "it's about being creative." Still, I resisted. It just wasn't my thing — or so I thought.

Then, the theater where Jordan was taking classes was hosting a "jam" (the improv equivalent of an open mic night), and Jordan really wanted to go, so I tagged along, happy to watch. The theater was only a 10-minute stroll from our apartment in Washington, DC's Adams Morgan neighborhood. Then, plot twist: When we got there, it became clear that there were more audience members (six? seven?)

than people who were there to get onstage (one? two?). I should note, this light attendance is typical for improv shows, as I would learn again and again in many a bar basement. In any case, the person who was there to emcee the event — a short, animated guy named Topher, who would go on to become my first improv teacher — turned to those of us in the audience and said, "What if we all just play improv games?"

And so, dear reader, we did.

A quick improv side note: What we did that night was something called short-form improv, which is all about playing improv games on stage (think "Whose Line Is It Anyway?"); the kind of improv I would go on to perform is something different, called long-form improv, which is more about storytelling — collaborating to spontaneously create a comedic play. Throughout this book, I'll be mining the lessons of long-form improv, since that's where most of my experience lies. The playfulness of short-form improv hooked me; the satisfying challenges I experienced practicing the skills of long-form improv, combined with the joy of play, are what kept me around.

Back to that fateful night in the black box theater: The game that turned me into a number two pencil was about telling one story from multiple perspectives. We all stood in a tight circle with our backs together. Somehow, we established that one of us was a student taking a standardized test. Then Topher pointed to someone else in the group, and that person decided they'd be the person proctoring the test and narrated what was happening from their perspective. By the time it got to me, I found myself saying, "I'm a number two pencil. Today is my time to shine."

Afterwards, walking home past the same trees and row homes I'd passed just a couple of hours earlier, I was a changed person. It was like the heavens had opened and a bright white light was shining down on me. Everything felt so *right*.

IMPROV IS FREEDOM

Growing up, acting was my very favorite thing, but before this moment, I hadn't been on stage in years. What happened that night, however, was more than someone with a love of performance coming home to herself. It was also a human being who lives in our tightly scripted world — "do this, don't do that"; "eat this, don't eat that"; "budget your money, schedule your time, watch what you say" — experiencing the bliss of freedom.

I want you to experience that bliss.

Again, life is nothing if not one big improv show. We think there are scripts we need to follow. But we are in fact sovereign beings who get to choose how we live.

**We are sovereign beings who get
to choose how we live.**

Jordan was right. Improv isn't about being funny, it's about being creative. Not "creative" in the sense of, "Wow, what a creative idea you just had," or "What a talented painter you are," but "creative" as in, engaged in the act of creating. Which is what all of us do, every single day: We create our lives when we decide who to spend time with, what activities to engage in, and what to say; what's more, we create our lives through *how* we do each of these things.

Shakespeare basically nailed it when he said that all the world's a stage, but he got an important detail wrong: We aren't "merely players" — we're improvisors, and there's nothing "mere" about it. We're making it up as we go — together. This book will show you how to improvise adulthood by being present and making one choice at a time, rather than striving for some distant notion of Success with a capital S. If the pandemic showed us anything, it's that we can't predict what comes our way; learning how to navigate the unexpected is far more valuable than putting together a rigid plan, one that has you thinking so much about your future that you can't feel whether your present is what you want it to be.

As improvisor, actor, writer, and producer Amy Poehler says in her book, *Yes, Please,*

> "The only thing we can depend on in life is that everything changes. The seasons, our partners, what we want and need. We hold hands with our high school friends and swear to never lose touch, and then we do. We scrape ice off our cars and feel like winter will never end, and it does...Change is the only constant. Your ability to navigate and tolerate change and its painful uncomfortableness directly correlates to your happiness and general well-being. See what I just did there? I saved you thousands of dollars on self-help books. If you can surf your life rather than plant your feet, you will be happier."

A NOTE ON AGE

I want to acknowledge that I am a 48-year-old writing a book that is first and foremost for those embarking on adulthood (though, if you're reading this in your 30s, 40s, 50s, or beyond, I welcome you! ... we're always creating our adulthoods, after all). The world has changed just a *wee* bit since I was starting out. When I graduated from college in 1998 (or "the late 1900s" as my daughter likes to call that period, or worse, "olden times"), the internet was brand new, and no one carried a cell phone; Jordan and I attended different schools and used prepaid calling cards and scheduled phone dates to keep in touch between visits. My sense of possible careers was eerily similar to the professions on display in Richard Scarry books: Firefighter! Doctor! Librarian! If you'd told me I was going to become a story coach who helped change makers and creative souls express themselves authentically, I would have been like, "Wait. That's a thing?!"

Now that we've established that I'm ancient, the question arises: Who am I to write a book that purports to offer relevant insight or guidance? Well, for one thing, I'm not suggesting that this book should be the only resource that can help you on your journey. That would be...strange. (I'm imagining you eschewing all other books that friends, librarians, and booksellers try to offer you: "No — only Amanda's!")

What's more, I believe passionately that everyone's story matters, not just the stories of famous people. And I believe that everyone's story has the potential to make a huge difference in someone else's life. The story coaching I do through Mighty Forces is predicated on these beliefs. In telling my story, I'm not suggesting that I'm the wisest expert in all the land; I'm sharing who I am and what I've learned in the hopes that reading my story helps you be you.

Plus, to state the obvious, growing up is something we've been doing since the dawn of humanity, and reading about other people's experiences, even if they unfolded back when we had to tape our favorite shows like suckers, may shed light on your own path. If you are a young person who craves a fulfilling, meaningful life, and you want to know how someone who has been in your shoes has created a life she loves, and what she's learned along the way — well, hi. I deeply hope this book offers you solace and inspiration as you carve your path in this weird, heartbreaking, beautiful world.

TIME FOR THE SHOW

Before every improv show, my teammates and I used to look each other in the eye and say, "I've got your back." Then someone would crank up the music and we'd run onstage like kids hyped up on juice boxes.

I've got your back.

Cue the music.

Let's do this.

SCENE 1

KNOW YOUR ORIGIN STORIES

"A scene is almost never about what the players think it's going to be about."

- Improv teachers and authors Del Close and Charna Halpern

Imagine: The crowd in the beer-scented basement awaits the improv show with eager anticipation. They demonstrate their enthusiasm by ~~smiling expectantly at the stage~~ staring at their phones. Each audience member is a character with a backstory — an origin story, if you will. And yet, in this moment, every single person in this audience has the potential to change their narrative.

Take, for example, that person in the baseball cap: Maybe their parents called them lazy, and they fell into acting the part; but maybe tonight is the night they decide to apply to the Peace Corps. They aren't lazy, they just weren't interested in the things they were taught in school, at least not the way they were taught to them. Truth is, they have a huge amount of curiosity about the world.

And that woman in the purple jacket — maybe she grew up in a community that expected girls to be polite at all costs; but maybe after the show, someone in line for the bathroom will say something that offends her, and she'll do something she's never done before, which is to say what she's thinking, out loud.

We don't know what will happen tonight, onstage or off. But we do know that whatever someone's story has been doesn't control what their story will be from this point forward.

ASKING "WHY?"

In some ways, my adulthood began when my parents instructed Jordan on how to butter a piece of bread.

We were eighteen years old, madly in love, and still learning to curb the PDA. They had very kindly invited us out to dinner at an Italian restaurant in Washington, DC — we lived in the Maryland suburbs, and going into the city was an occasion. We took our seats. Jordan reached for a piece of bread from the basket at the center of the table and began buttering it.

"Oh," one of my parents said (I can't remember which one), "it's actually more polite to butter each individual bite." They showed him how to put a little dab of butter on the side of his bread plate, then tear off one small piece of bread at a time, butter it, and eat it.

They meant well, but I was mortified. Jordan was curious.

"Why?" he asked.

Why?

I never asked "why?"

Someone told me it was the right way to do it, so I did it.

By asking "why?" about something as inconsequential as table manners, Jordan woke something up inside me; something that would soon have me asking questions like, "What's the real purpose of going to college?"

But I'm getting ahead of myself.

Back to the bread.

"It's just considered more polite," my parents said. We went back to our meal and had a nice time. But something shifted then, like a tectonic plate. With his simple query, Jordan had made me realize that we don't have to just accept the stories we're told; we can ask "why?" And when we do, we may realize the answer doesn't satisfy us, and neither does the story — or script — of which it's a part.

THE POWER OF SAYING "YES, AND"

A willingness to question the status quo is essential to improvising your life: After all, improvisors don't follow scripts, they create them. But this doesn't mean that improvising is about rejecting everything that other people suggest or recommend; in fact, the key to effective improvisation isn't rejection at all — it's acceptance.

Let's take an example: Your scene partner says, "Nice day to be on the moon." What are your choices? You could say "no": "No it's not. It's a shitty day on Jupiter." Well, now you've denied the reality that your scene partner began to establish, so instead of advancing the scene, you've taken us back to zero. Maybe it seems funny to be disagreeable, or interesting, but the most experienced improvisors know, that's a cheap path to getting a laugh, one that undermines the scene and keeps it from becoming comedic gold.

What happens if you say "yes" instead? "Yep, nice day on the moon." Well, that's very congenial of you — you've accepted your scene partner's offer, which puts you on the path to creating a shared reality — but you haven't helped to advance the scene.

What if you say "yes, and"?

"Nice day to be on the moon," your scene partner says, and you reply, "Oh honey, being here with you is the best anniversary present ever." That line alone may not be a laugh riot, but you've accepted the reality your scene partner initiated, and you've built on it — now we know, you're not just two random people on the moon for no reason, you're a couple celebrating your anniversary. And we also know that your character is grateful and affectionate.

Saying "yes" doesn't mean you agree; it means you *accept*. For example, if someone told you, "You're flighty, you better find someone stable to marry who can pay the bills," saying "yes" would mean accepting the truth that someone told you that. It was said, as hurtful and problematic as it may have felt. Now you get to choose the "and." "Yes, they said I was flighty, and, I don't believe that; I plan to pay my own way in life, not rely on someone else."

I want you to start looking at the stories that the world has fed you up to this point, and that you have digested, and notice that they are mental constructs. When you start "yes, and"-ing what's right in front of you — instead of getting distracted by stories in your head about how things are "supposed" to go and allowing them to guide you — you realize you are the pilot of your life, rather than a passenger.

Just as superheroes have origin stories, we all have stories we internalize growing up that shape our lives. These stories come from family members, teachers, the media we consume, all of it. Some are explicit, others implicit. These origin stories become like a pair of glasses that both enhance and restrict our vision: We easily spot proof that our stories are true and are quick to overlook evidence that contradicts our truth. And so we move through the world.

Let me share more of my own origin story to help illustrate how the narratives that surround us can shape the choices we make.

ONCE UPON A TIME IN ROCKVILLE, MARYLAND...

I am fortunate that, growing up in the safety of a Rockville, Maryland cul-de-sac, I had supportive parents with whom I was extremely close. They imparted many stories to me, including through their own examples, that helped make me who I am today: confident (no small feat for a woman in our culture), capable, and, I'd like to think, compassionate. My mother, for example, was Wonder Woman in shoulder pads: A self-possessed health care executive who made me feel like I was the most important thing in her world, and who cooked us a healthy dinner every single night (except the one night a week that we ordered from Seven Seas Chinese restaurant — their veggie dumplings are still unrivaled, in my book). And my father, an accountant, was a steady, loving presence. He had the soul of a poet, something I wouldn't realize until much later; all I knew growing up was that he always really listened to me, and, together with my mom, gave me the gift of believing that the things I said mattered.

But of course, as the poet Philip Larkin so wisely observed, "They fuck you up, your mum and dad," and there's no getting around it; as a parent now myself, I know I'm unintentionally feeding my daughter origin stories that she will need to untangle as an adult. And so, my parents, like all parents, also imparted stories that ended up hurting me; or the way I metabolized those stories hurt me. Stories like: The dream of being an actress when you grow up is just that — a dream — with no hope of becoming a reality.

When I continued to talk about my dream of an acting career well into high school, there was a moment when my dad said, "Well, maybe after college, Amanda should spend a year in New York City to see if she can make it." He was trying to be supportive but notice how what he said reveals a belief (a story, if you will) that "making it" as an actor is like winning the lottery — a turn of fate randomly awarded, as opposed to an outcome towards which one might steadily and constructively apply oneself. His attitude was understandable, as he himself had heard far more stories about starving artists than about artists who thrived.

My mom did not like my dad's New York plan, and at the time, her disapproval was enough to shut me down. Only many years later did I learn that my mother is an incredibly talented visual artist who chose not to pursue art professionally, in large part because she had seen her own mother struggle financially to raise three children as a single parent; that certainly explains her lack of enthusiasm about me pursuing an acting career. I wonder how things might have been different if my family had known first-hand a number of artists who were able to support themselves through their work — something that Adult Me now knows is eminently possible, if not easy...but then, what's easy?

Experiencing the power of stories to shape our sense of what is and isn't possible, and to affect the courage we do or do not have when pursuing our dreams, had a lasting effect on me. Today I'm passionate about people sharing stories about the work they do, and why they do it, because I know that one person's story can so easily become part of someone else's mental map of what is and isn't available to them.

One person's story can so easily become part of someone else's mental map of what is and isn't available to them.

My path to acting was shut down because I let it be — understandable for a compliant 17-year-old, but ultimately, my choice. This is an important part of reckoning with your origin stories: The point isn't to blame everyone else and feel like a victim; the point isn't "blame" at all. Yes, you were a child, or an adolescent, and the adults in your life had more power than you; what's also true is that the details of who you are, in spirit and in genes, influenced how you received and applied the stories that other people fed you. Another person could have gone through the same set of experiences as you did, been surrounded by the same influences, and internalized different stories, made different choices.

QUESTIONING YOUR SOURCES

As I edged closer to college age, I continued to internalize a number of sad, limiting stories from various sources around the idea of pursuing a creative life, including: Creativity isn't lucrative, and you can't support yourself as an artist; creativity isn't for people who are good at school (smart, straight-A students like me pursued more "serious" and "impressive" things than acting careers); and, the doozy: creativity is selfish.

For this last one, I blamed the Post-it note.

Let me explain: When I was 17, my friend Kate, whom I met in kindergarten, suggested we take a spontaneous road trip down to the University of Virginia, where Jordan was attending a songwriting camp. "Heck yes," I said. When we got there, I went straight to Jordan's dorm, where we quickly began making out (on the ride home, Kate told me it looked like an octopus had been sucking on my neck). At some point, I came up for air and ventured down the hall to use the ladies' room — and that's when I saw it, on the back of the stall door: A yellow Post-it note that said, in an unadorned scrawl, "Self-expression is not a virtue."

Well, fuck.

That hit me like a gut punch. It would be like someone saying, "You are not actually a human being" — that's how ingrained in me it was that, in fact, self-expression *was* a virtue. As I've said, acting and creative writing were my passions. In elementary school my report card was filled with Os for Outstanding, except for when it came to raising my hand before I spoke, which was always S for Satisfactory; when I had something to say, I felt like I would burst if I didn't get to say it. In high school, I took a creative writing class and my teacher, Mrs. Wilchek, with her signature scent of rosewater, told us that the 10 minutes she gave us to write in our journals were 10 minutes just for us, a time when no one else's expectations of us mattered. I came to equate self-expression with freedom.

But there I was, in the loo, confronted with the idea that expressing myself was not inherently virtuous. So that meant...maybe freedom wasn't virtuous, either? And I was nothing if not compelled to be virtuous — a "good girl," nice, polite, straight As, thin — all the things my culture encouraged.

I became uneasy about my appetite for self-expression. That Post-it note shook my faith in the value of my own voice, and it set me back for years. When I took a series of sociology classes in college, my sheltered bubble of an affluent suburban upbringing began to pop. As I learned about inner-city poverty and the AIDS epidemic, the idea of expressing personal feelings felt self-indulgent at best. The only art that was worthy, in my mind, was art that raised people's awareness of something important; my benchmark at the time was *Schindler's List*.

Soon my philosophy pretty much boiled down to: Make *Schindler's List* or keep it to yourself.

Fortunately, the story that my opinions mattered was not squashed by the story that expression was not a virtue. I still spoke my mind; I was still confident, just not when it came to creative expression.

All because of a Post-it note, and how strongly it reinforced fears that were already latent inside me.

Word to the wise: Do not let a Post-it note from God knows who — in a bathroom stall, no less — dictate your destiny!

AN OPENING OFFER

In my early 20s, Kate was in a toxic relationship with a mentally ill man who periodically refused to take the medication that kept him from doing things like writing in a giant scrawl all over their walls or, worse, disappearing into the city for days on end. One night, as we sat talking about it, I said, "I don't get it — at some point, don't you just get mad? I would get *mad*." And without missing a beat, she said, "That's because you have strong self-esteem."

Notice how her words reveal a script that she was carrying around.

These scripts — they're everywhere, man. Invisible, sometimes helpful, sometimes debilitating; some propel us forward, and some hold us back. Which is why the first step to improvising a fulfilling adult life is simply and profoundly to take stock of the scripts that are guiding you in this world, scripts you are unwittingly following. Becoming aware of harmful inputs won't magically eliminate them, but over time, awareness will be like medicine that helps you make authentic choices — choices that comprise the story, or life, that you want most.

Think of the stories you were raised with as an opening offer. Your job is to look them square in the eyes and say, just like an improvisor would: "Yes, and." In other words: "Yes, that has been the story I've believed up until now. And I am going to live my way into my own story." Let go of what you thought your life had to look like and respond to the life that is actually happening.

Think of the stories you were raised with as an opening offer.

In improv, as in life, this is a hard lesson to learn. Early on, I used to enter a scene with a strong idea of what it would be about: "Ooh! We should be on a first date." But when my scene partner inevitably said something that veered from my mental script, I'd be stuck. I'd try to shoehorn the information they shared to fit my preconceived idea, and that never went well. It derailed the scene, making it a power struggle instead of a collaboration.

Things go so much better when we collaborate with life, rather than fight it. That doesn't mean we're doormats, or suckers. It means that when something happens that we don't like, we understand that saying "no" gets us stuck — no matter how much we say "no," the thing we don't like has happened, and we can't make it un-happen... whereas saying "yes, and" helps us move forward, and beyond.

REFLECT

It probably won't surprise you that I encourage you to consider what scripts you may be carrying with you. This will be a process that unfolds over time, not something you figure out all in one sitting! Maybe create a Notes file on your phone, or fire up a Google Doc, and jot down new insights as they pop into your brain; or keep a special journal for this purpose.

Also, and this is important: Your job is to write down whatever comes up for you, not to worry about getting it "right." No one else will see your answers; no one is grading you. Consider that for these questions, as well as the ones at the end of each subsequent chapter, getting it "right" might not even be possible.

Without further ado, here are some questions to consider:

- What did your parents or other primary caregivers teach you — either implicitly, by their own example, or explicitly, through what they told you — about what is and is not possible in an adult life? Consider these themes: fulfillment, work, dreams, creativity, money, safety, health, community, and success.

- What about the stories you imbibed through books, TV, movies, podcasts, social media — what did they teach you was possible and impossible, realistic and unrealistic, honorable and dishonorable?

- Which of the stories you internalized about adulthood serve you well, and which do not? Where do you agree, or disagree?

- What if you considered these origin stories as opening offers, or scene initiations made by the adults in your life, and thought of yourself as their scene partner, instead of an audience member? How might you find ways to "yes, and" your origin stories?

As I set off for college, my parents encouraged me to use my time there to figure out what I wanted to do with my life. But after so many years inside an education system that conditioned me to follow the rules and to seek gold stars, I lacked the tools to make choices for myself. I had no idea what I actually wanted (except, of course, to act, which I had internalized was not a valid choice). As I began my first semester at the University of Pennsylvania, I continued performing the expected scenes, much like a hamster unaware of life beyond the wheel — until suddenly, it felt like that wheel was rolling out of the cage, out the front door, and into oncoming traffic.

SCENE 2
GET OFF THE HAMSTER WHEEL

"The only safe thing is to take a chance."

- Improvisor, actor, writer, and director Elaine May

Back to the beer-scented improv theater.

Remember the woman in the purple jacket, waiting in line for the bathroom after the show? Let's call her Izzy. Well, Izzy was raised to be polite, no matter what, and got signals from not only her parents and grandparents but also her teachers and the media that her job, as a woman, was to smooth over any uncomfortable moments. If a male teacher made an inappropriate remark about her outfit, her job was to smile and not make a big deal about it. If her gruff uncle said something obnoxious at Thanksgiving, it was up to her and the other women at the table to keep the peace.

But on this night, standing in this line, something shifts inside of Izzy. Maybe it's the improv show she just saw, the way the actors put themselves out there; if they could risk falling flat on their faces in front of a live audience, what risks might she be able to take?

The person behind her is making offensive comments about one of the performers — talking about how fat she is, how lucky she is that the theater let someone who looked like her on stage.

"Her body size is actually none of your business," Izzy hears herself saying. "And by the way, I thought she was the funniest one up there."

Saying what she's thinking is new for Izzy, and as the words come out of her mouth, she has the feeling of waking from a trance. If she can respond to rude people in line for the bathroom, what else might she be capable of?

This is what improvising does: it wakes us up to the power we have inside of us to make a choice, and then another one. It reminds us that we're creating a script, not following one imposed on us by someone else.

CATERPILLAR: "THIS IS HARD"

Now that you're becoming more aware of the invisible scripts that are guiding your life — in ways large and small, helpful and decidedly unhelpful — I want to share what the process of choosing your own script can look like. It's not unlike being a caterpillar who suddenly finds itself in the dramatic, painful, beautiful process of becoming a butterfly, except no one has promised that butterfly status lies ahead... it just feels like everything is really hard and ill-fitting.

My transition from cheerful high school student to morose college student was remarkably swift.

My high school was full of wonderful, smart, creative humans. I know many people hate this time of life, but I loved it. My parents had suggested I enroll in the International Baccalaureate program, which turned out to be a godsend. I felt a tremendous sense of belonging, something I took for granted the way you can take good eyesight for granted until, suddenly, you have to strain to see what once was crystal clear.

In my first year at the University of Pennsylvania, or "Penn," as many people call it, the whole world felt out of focus. And I couldn't find a pair of glasses that worked.

Shortly before graduation, my high school writing teacher, Mrs. Wilchek, she of the scent of rose water, pulled me aside in the hall. "I really don't see you at Penn," she said. I think she was trying to save me. This is one of those "Sliding Doors" moments...What if I'd listened? But I didn't.

Fast forward to the first week of college: It's freshman orientation, and I'm sitting in the middle of the quad on the balcony of an old stone building. Next to me and spread out on the lawn in front of me are hundreds of students. I am looking up at the moon.

I am alone.

Despite being an outgoing person, something about the forced fun of orientation week left me feeling alienated, rather than welcomed. I felt no chemistry with my roommate; I ate meals with her and some other people from my dorm, but never felt fully at ease.

If this were a movie, now is when you'd see a montage of me spending freshman year trying one activity after another, in an attempt to find my people. I went to a meeting of the literary magazine, but I didn't know anyone and felt like a random fly on the wall. Same thing when I tried joining the newspaper. I went to an open house for a bunch of different drama clubs, didn't click with anyone, felt disconnected, and left.

If this were a movie, now is when you'd see a montage of me spending freshman year trying one activity after another.

From my vantage point over 20 years later, I can see that if I'd had a buddy attending these things with me, or if the people running the clubs had had a better idea of how to make new people feel included, everything could have been different. But they didn't, and I was buddy-less, and I continued to struggle.

Eventually, my mother persuaded me to try Greek life. I *really* didn't want to — it did not seem like my thing — but she made a strong case, and I was running out of other options. I rushed and ended up pledging Chi Omega (for those of you for whom Greek life is foreign, that basically means I auditioned and then I got the part). It was because of that choice that I ended up meeting my three best college friends, people whose friendship continues to this day. But the whole sorority thing never felt right to me; I'd attend events with my "sisters" and just feel like a fish out of water. I wasn't interested in the things they were interested in. A big factor was that I was dating Jordan long-distance; I was more interested in writing and exploring the city and connecting with people over shared creative interests than I was in meeting dudes or partying. (Back then, the assumption was that everyone in the sorority was straight; I wonder how many of those people weren't actually straight, but were going through the motions of what they thought was expected of them? ...in other words, following a script.)

ONE SAD PUPA

Fast forward, now, to my junior year. I'm walking down Walnut Street in Philadelphia, and I am crying. I have been haunted for weeks by a feeling of just going through the motions of my life, and now, it's a random weekday morning, and I can't stop the tears. I pass the Cinnabon, the Gap, chain stores that feel as impersonal and separate from me as my entire college experience so far. I get myself back to my on-campus apartment and call Kate. "You need to get on a train," she tells me, "And go home."

And I do.

In the rearview mirror, I see now that what I was experiencing was part existential crisis; part clinical depression, which it would take another near decade to diagnose; and part being deeply in love with someone who went to a different school, several hours away. Notice, here, how making choices that are true for you — such as dating Jordan long-distance all through college — can appear "wrong" to people on the outside, at the time ("Why don't you date around? You're only young once!"), only to inspire people later ("Oh my gosh, you guys have been together *how* long? You should give motivational talks about being in a successful marriage!").

Back to the existential part: I couldn't shake the feeling that there was this enormous gap between why people said they were at Penn and why they seemed to actually be there. What they said: "To get an education." What I saw: People gunning for good grades in order to get a good job — and by "good," I mean, lucrative and "impressive" (that is to say, at a well-known company), not necessarily meaningful or fulfilling. Many students had parents who had gone to Penn, and now here they were, graduating straight into jobs at places like McKinsey & Company that paid 21-year-olds $100,000 a year. It was like a privilege factory, where so many of the other girls dressed identically, a parade of black pants weaving through campus like a trail of ants. Ants work hard, but they are not independent thinkers.

I'm sure this is an unfair generalization, but it's absolutely how it felt to me, at the time.

I couldn't shake the feeling that there was this enormous gap between why people said they were at Penn and why they seemed to actually be there.

I'd recently read *Zen and the Art of Motorcycle Maintenance* by Robert Pirsig; in it, he writes that "removing grades exposes a huge vacuum in our system of education." That hit me like a gut punch. I became aware of myself as a hamster on a wheel. Take me off the wheel, and what the hell would I do with myself? What was I actually doing here, at this institution that cost my parents $32,000 a year? I wrote an op-ed for the school paper calling out the gap between the reasons we claimed to be at Penn, and my felt experience of why people were *actually* there. I'm sure it warmed my parents' hearts to read it, as they continued working hard to pay to send me to this place that made me feel alienated and alone.

At home in my childhood bedroom in Rockville, I looked at my pink and seafoam green decor and felt...lame. What was wrong with me? Why did these things bother me, that didn't bother other people? Jordan went to the University of Maryland, so being home meant I could see him more. I remember sitting at a party with his a cappella group and just feeling so, so *sad*.

I thought about transferring to another school. I went to visit Kate at Wesleyan, in Connecticut, where there was a strong creative vibe. Her friends cooked dinner while I was there, gathering around a small kitchen table and drinking wine out of coffee mugs. They were musicians and filmmakers; Kate herself was studying costume design. They also did a lot of drugs, and it terrified me. I felt on the one hand, like I was with my people, and, on the other hand, like I was a self-conscious square who would never fit in.

Meanwhile, my mother wasn't having it. She called up the advisory office at Penn and declared, "Hello, I sent you my talented, happy child and she's miserable and left in the middle of the semester, what do you have to say?" In hindsight, I see how she was modeling how I could advocate for myself; years later, I'd become a fierce advocate for my own daughter. Anyway, she got someone on the phone who asked, "Why isn't Amanda an English major? She should be an English major.

All the creative kids are English majors. Not to mention, I'm looking at her transcript, and all her electives are in the English department." My mom passed these messages along, and soon I was talking to the advisor. "But an English degree is impractical," I argued. It was hard being a liberal arts student at Penn, where three of the four undergraduate schools were explicitly pre-professional (business, engineering, and nursing); it felt illogical to me for my parents to pay so much tuition for me to...read books. That's why I was a Communications major — it was practical. "Be that as it may," this advisor told me, "The English department is where you will fit in."

Ok, I thought. I'd rather be the more liberal, creative one in a conservative environment, than the more conservative (lifestyle-wise) person in a more liberal environment like Wesleyan. So, I went back.

But this time, everything was different.

I was, as Alicia Keys might put it, a girl on fire; improvising one choice that veered away from the script I thought I was supposed to be following unleashed a hunger for more.

BUTTERFLY TIME, BABY

It turned out, I'd taken so many high-level English seminars as electives, that now I had to take a bunch of intro-level classes just to fulfill the requirements of the major. In Intro to British literature, we read the English mystery plays, which are based on Bible stories. Our teacher assigned us to write an essay, and something inside of me was like, "Naw." I went to her office hours and said, "I can write this essay. But I've written a million essays like it. Could I write a play instead?" And, to her immense credit, she said yes.

I was literally writing my own scripts. I was saying, "Yes, and" years before I ever set foot on an improv stage.

I wrote a modern take on the "immaculate conception" in which Joseph doesn't believe Mary that her pregnancy is a miracle; he insists she must have cheated on him. She feels betrayed by him, and by God, telling God she never asked for a child. My teacher had us do a readthrough in class. Then I wrote another play, this time a modern take on Noah's ark, in which his wife thinks he's bizarre for listening to God and building this giant ark in Philly's Rittenhouse Square; and then she drowns. Again, we read it as a class. It was so validating. And invigorating. And, dare I say, fun.

What did fun have to do with anything?! You worked hard, you got good grades; when had anyone said anything about enjoyment? The seed was planted: When I took the reins and brought creativity to bear — when I improvised — I had a better time; and I liked it.

When I took the reins and brought creativity to bear — when I improvised — I had a better time; and I liked it.

I also started an independent study that first semester back that became a seminal experience for me. Our professors espoused John Dewey's educational philosophy and encouraged using students' questions to drive our learning. We each came up with a core question that we wanted to answer through a project we would then design. My question was something to the effect of, "What would it take to help more Penn students have a meaningful college experience?" I ended up proposing a writing course for first-year students designed to get people to actively reflect on what they wanted out of college; the syllabus then supported them in mapping out creative ways to achieve their goals. For example, if a student were interested in learning about politics and filmmaking, maybe a professor could help guide them to an internship at the local PBS station, which produced documentary films about the social issues of the day.

(Years later, I would be drawn to the democratic school model for my daughter; so often, seeds get planted in young adulthood that become growth we nurture throughout our entire adult lives.)

I was so proud of my proposal. It meant so much to me, and I really believed in the power of what I was suggesting. Looking back, I can see that this was a moment when so many themes of my adult life were born — most importantly, a focus on intentionality and agency, and on turning my own pain into positive offerings for others. Between this independent project, and the playwriting, I was learning that I didn't have to just take what the world offered me. I could carve my own path. And it felt *good*. Yes, and...

Near the end of my senior year, the head of the English department asked to meet with me. I sat facing her dark wooden desk as she told me that I would be inducted into the Phi Beta Kappa society. I assumed, at first, that it was because of my good grades, and I wasn't that excited; it was nice, but not particularly meaningful. Then she said that the nominating committee was particularly impressed with my independent approach to my education. Holy shit. I'd acted on my instincts, I'd shaped things in a way that made them more meaningful for me, and *that* was being honored?! *Wow.* I was honored, indeed.

This was such a pivotal moment for me, as I got ready to head out into my adult life. Some new part of me was waking up, and when other people recognized it, I felt seen in a way that no "A+" had ever done.

LEARNING TO FEEL "YES"

Going off-script can be grueling (see: all the angst I felt for most of my time in college, crying in the middle of the day, a leave of absence from school) but is, so often, deeply rewarding and joyful (see: how happy I was after I came back to school and started doing things my way); it makes accomplishments feel more meaningful. For years,

Penn felt like "no" in every fiber of my being. If you've ever felt like you don't belong or like it's hard to be in a certain environment or social group, then you know what I'm talking about. And then suddenly, writing those plays, proposing a new class that could help other people avoid the unhappiness I'd experienced — all of that felt very much like "yes."

Transcending the scripts that don't serve you requires a willingness and ability to listen to what feels like "yes" to you, and what feels like "no" — and to act to those feelings. Improvisors do this when they perform, learning to listen to when it feels right to make a certain move. The actors can't stop the show, go off stage, and make a quick Excel spreadsheet to analyze the situation! But, with practice, they can learn to trust their instincts, moving by feel towards the story and rhythm that is there, that is unfolding as they and their scene partners create something that wasn't there before.

If you can learn to listen to what feels true for you, and to act on it, you will feel at home in yourself. There is no better feeling.

REFLECT

Take a minute and ask yourself if you know what "yes" and "no" feel like. You're not looking for intellectual responses here — you're noticing *what it feels like in your body* when something is right, and when something is wrong.

Some questions to consider:

- What is an example of a time or place where you felt like, "I don't fit here, this isn't right for me"?

- What is an example of a time or place where, by contrast, you felt like, "Hell yeah. It's easy to be here, I can relax and be myself"?

- If you're struggling to come up with examples, a reminder not to worry about "getting it right" — just make a guess: "I think this situation was a 'no' for me, and this one was a 'yes.'" You will not be graded! The point is to continue practicing applying the ideas from this book to your own life; there's no expectation that everything will click 100% right away.

We'll talk more about feeling into what's right for ourselves in Chapter 8 — really noting the physical sensations that accompany "yes" and "no" — but for now, just begin to bring awareness to this idea of how "yes" and "no" register for you.

I graduated from college feeling pretty darn happy and proud of myself. Then, a few months later, I started my first job, and there was that gap again, between what was expected, and what felt right.

SCENE 3

DISCOVER THE ~~THING~~ THINGS YOU WANT TO DO

"The only real mistake here is ignoring the inner voice."

- Improv teachers and authors Del Close and Charna Halpern

The next night, Izzy is back at the theater, high on the feeling she had after last night's show. She wants more of whatever that was injected into her veins. As the actors take the stage, one of them announces that the theater offers improv classes, and that there are sign-up sheets in the lobby. Izzy considers: Should she sign up? "No, that's crazy," she tells herself. "I'm a web designer, not an actor. And there's so much going on at work, not to mention my sister's wedding..."

And yet, something inside of Izzy feels like taking this class is exactly what she's meant to do, even if it makes no logical sense. After the show ends, she lingers in the lobby, hovering near the sign-up sheet. Finally, she mutters, "What the hell," and adds her name to the list.

In life, as in improv, we serve ourselves best when we follow the yes.

FIRST JOB: EPIC FAIL

As I embarked on my post-college life, I felt like a plug without a socket. Just as I'd struggled to put myself in the box of a major, putting myself in the box of one of the career paths apparent to me felt... wrong. No job sounded like a fit.

At a campus job fair the spring before graduation, recruiters from a healthcare research company had billed themselves as the perfect fit for the intellectual college grad who wasn't quite sure what she wanted to do (check); they said it was an especially great place for people who loved to write (double check). I submitted my resume and was invited to an interview.

Picture this: I'm sitting in the sterile, glimmering offices of a healthcare research company located next door to Washington, DC's infamous Watergate hotel. A self-serious 20-something in a sweater vest leans forward and asks:

"If you could be a consultant to an unborn child, would you advise them to be born today, or 2,000 years ago?"

Um.

I check to see if he's kidding; he's not.

I consider the man-child's question. I am a confused college senior who is increasingly panicked about finding a job. As far as I know, these kinds of questions are par for the course in the working world.

I clarify: "Do you mean, in the context of healthcare?"

"No, just in general," he replies, gazing at me through his tortoise-shell glasses.

I say something about life seeming simpler in the past, to which he responds, "No. That's the wrong answer." (And here I thought it was a matter of opinion!) "The right answer," he tells me, "Is *today*. Because we have air conditioning. And television."

He proceeds to elaborate on his theory of why these are the two most significant innovations in human history; the chance for him to pontificate, it becomes clear, is the whole reason for the question in the first place.

Despite my egregious ignorance, the company would later offer me the job. And I'd take it, without enthusiasm, knowing I had to do something to earn money. My parents made it clear that I could live at home the summer after graduation, but after that, I'd have to pay rent. I thought, "This definitely isn't my dream job, but I don't know what is, and maybe this will at least get me closer to the thing I want to do."

A COMEDIAN SPEAKS TRUTH

"The thing I want to do" — this was language I'd picked up from the comedian Conan O'Brien when he came to speak at Penn during my senior year. I had a major crush on him (nothing was more attractive to a 21-year-old me than a sense of humor — funny was like a sexy musk), so I hurried to pick up a free ticket from the campus organization that was giving them out. But I didn't hurry enough, and they were sold out by the time I arrived. This fit my profile: Being on time was never my strong suit. In high school, I was the straight-A student who got detention for being chronically late to first period (incidentally, the class for which I was late was taught by, wait for it, Mr. Early).

Poor Josh Greenberg, who relied on me as his ride to school.

"Um, Amanda?" he'd ask, tentatively. "Do you think maybe you could, um, try to get here a little earlier?"

"Yes, yes, of course, I'm so sorry," I'd say, and then, in the manner of shampoo application, we would rinse and repeat the whole scenario again and again.

And again.

But Conan (in my mind, we were on a first-name basis) was my *favorite,* and I was desperate to get a ticket. I wouldn't take no for an answer. That night, as people lined up outside the auditorium where he would be speaking, I went up and down the line of strangers, offering them $20 for their free ticket. At the time, this felt like a tremendous amount of money (even now, $20 for a $0 ticket is a pretty nice markup), but there was no question in my mind that it was worth it. You might say, it felt like "yes." And so, no matter how many "noes" I encountered, I didn't give up.

Finally, someone sold me their ticket.

I knew I loved Conan's humor, but what I didn't know, before that day, was that he had wisdom to share that I would still think about over 20 years later. He stood on that stage, and instead of just telling jokes, spoke very earnestly about how, at job after job, he had ultimately moved on when it stopped being "the thing he wanted to do."

Now, to my current ear, that sounds incredibly privileged — and it is. Most people can't afford to just leave a job when the spirit moves them. Then again, most people who *can* afford to leave, stay. Which reminds me of a quote from Keith Johnstone, famed improv teacher and author of *Impro*:

> "People with dull lives often think that their lives are dull by chance. In reality, everyone chooses more or less what kind of events will happen to them by their conscious patterns of blocking and yielding. A student objected to this view by saying, 'But you don't choose your life. Sometimes, you

are at the mercy of people who push you around.' I said, 'Do you avoid such people?' 'Oh!' she said, 'I see what you mean.'"

The idea of stopping something when it no longer serves you might sound like it belongs squarely in the "duh" category. But I think you know: It's not that easy. And for a room full of overachievers programmed to meet other people's expectations, the idea of following our feelings — of treating feelings as legitimately as thoughts — was radical. At least, it was radical for me.

In the story he told, Conan wasn't just leaving dead-end temp jobs; he eventually left his job writing for "The Simpsons" — an opportunity many people would kill to have — for no reason other than that it no longer felt right. And against all odds, he ended up hosting a late-night television show. *That* felt right. He found the thing he wanted to do.

I left the auditorium that night feeling giddy with excitement and hope. I, too, would find the thing I wanted to do. But first, my friend Karen and I would figure out which nearby restaurant Conan was eating at, and sit a couple of tables away, gawking and trying to catch his eye, to no avail.

What I can see now that I couldn't see then, is that I did in fact know what I wanted to do, I just didn't think I was allowed to do it; maybe you can relate. I wanted to act, and I wanted to pursue dramatic writing (writing those plays had sparked something inside me). I even found the nerve to apply to an MFA program in dramatic writing; when I didn't get in, I took that to mean, "You aren't good at this," when of course, what it really meant was, simply, "This program — the one program, of many, to which you chose to apply — didn't choose to accept you."

**I did in fact know what I wanted to do, I
just didn't think I was allowed to do it.**

Why I persisted in scoring a Conan ticket, but gave up so quickly when pursuing writing, has to do with how possible each thing seemed to me. That MFA program felt like a big-ol' "yes," but I was still fighting off those scripts I'd grown up with, scripts that told me it should probably be "no." It would take time and practice to learn to follow "yes" even when it went against what I expected about how the world worked.

So, I went back to approaching my career as if it were a Rubik's Cube, one where the goal was to find fulfilling work that wasn't the actual work I wanted to do. A complicated game, indeed.

LEAVERS GONNA LEAVE?

On my first day at the healthcare research company, my manager told me and the other hapless recruits that our productivity would be measured in points. I kid you not: Here at this "think tank" for "intellectuals," we had to earn five productivity points every week. Different kinds of assignments yielded different point values. "Writing," it turned out, meant filling in boilerplate reports with information gleaned through literature reviews and phone interviews that they scripted for us. I remember this company loved the word "aforementioned." If you veered from the script, you were directed right back to it. I felt like an automaton. In staff meetings, managers said things like, "Let's double click on that idea."

Here's an idea: Let's not.

Unless writing angry poetry in corporate meetings was "the thing I wanted to do," it became increasingly clear to me that I needed to move on. But I judged myself harshly for the impulse; remember, I had spent my entire life overachieving and getting praised for my ability to leverage my intellect to perform an assigned task and was new to the idea of trusting my feelings. None of my friends were leaving their jobs, even if they found them uninspiring. If they could suck it up, why couldn't I? Quitting something didn't feel brave — it felt lame. And I worried it was becoming a pattern.

It was one thing to leave Penn and come back on my own terms. But now, to leave my first post-college job, less than a year in? What was I? A...leaver?

To go from the self-actualized, independent, mission-driven way that my college career culminated, to "let's double click on that idea" and earning productivity points, was a depressing shock, to say the least. Was the way of being that led to my Phi Beta Kappa recognition only lauded in an academic setting? Out in the "real world," was the mature thing to do just to fall in line?

After less than a year at the Company of Doom, Jordan and I got married. Enough people gave us checks as wedding gifts that I saw an escape route. We were on our honeymoon in Cancun, which our wedding party had, incredibly, bankrolled — Jordan graduated from college with $7 in the bank, and my entry-level salary left no room for savings or extras; Jordan had a solid job lined up, but he hadn't started it yet. Without my maid of honor, Wendy's, incredible creativity in pulling the trip together for us, our honeymoon would have consisted of eating Ben & Jerry's on our sofa (which, let's be real, is still one of my favorite things to do).

So, there we were, sitting on the beach in Playa del Carmen, Mexico, when I declared that I wanted to quit my job as soon as we got back. Only a few weeks out of college, the sweet man I married nodded supportively. If I said it would work out, he trusted me; he believed in my "yes." This would be the first of many leaps we would make together.

Back in the States, I gave my two weeks' notice. It felt right, and exhilarating, and embarrassing, all at once. Listening to the voice inside me that said, "This can't be all there is," took courage, though at the time, it also felt like I was broken, or wrong, for not fitting into something that seemed to work for so many other people.

FOLLOWING BREADCRUMBS

As a freshly out-of-work newlywed, I reflected on what I could learn from my time at Productivity Inc. so that I didn't end up in such an ill-fitting situation again. I decided that I wanted a job that heavily featured creativity and communication. This felt like the kindergarten level of knowing what I wanted to do with my life, but hey, we all start in kindergarten, and knowing something was better than knowing nothing. Sometimes, recognizing that something is a "yes" feels more like following breadcrumbs on a trail to "yes," than feeling "yes" resonate in every fiber of your being. "Creativity" and "communication" were my breadcrumbs.

Sometimes, recognizing that something is a "yes" feels more like following breadcrumbs on a trail to "yes," than feeling "yes" resonate in every fiber of your being.

One day, I was poking around online when I found a woman's resume that caught my attention. Keep in mind, this was pre-LinkedIn, so seeing a stranger's resume was rare. I was struck by how the picture hers painted actually looked...interesting. Her name was Jude, and she'd worked as a producer at NPR and the Discovery Channel, and now she was with Washingtonpost.com. I sniffed: Was that a whiff of "creativity and communication"?

I emailed her to say, "Hey, your resume looks interesting, could I buy you a cup of coffee for an informational interview?" She immediately wrote back to say, "Yes."

A week or so later, I was standing in the black marble lobby of the suburban Virginia building where Washingtonpost.Newsweek Interactive kept its offices. Jude appeared, with a stylish bob and intelligent eyes, and introduced herself. I was ready to head out to a coffee shop nearby when she said, "Wanna come see the newsroom?"

The next thing I knew, we were in an elevator going up. Jude turned to me: "Remind me, are you a coder, or a content person?" "Um, a content person," I replied. I wondered if my answer was unethical, since I had no professional experience having anything to do with website content, unless you counted that academic department website I'd briefly been paid to update in college? Then again, I was a lifelong writer and recent English major, and I knew HTML because a prescient professor, Al Filreis, had required it, and I'd created a website for his class in which I presented my ideas about community, so — saying I was a "content person" was, on some level at least, true.

The doors opened. We entered the newsroom. As we walked around, Jude introduced me to more than a dozen people as "her friend, Amanda, the content producer." I interviewed for five jobs that day. *Five.* Keep in mind that this was during the dot-com boom. I had a degree from the University of Pennsylvania (which, as we've covered, I'd mostly hated, but the glossy name still helped on my resume), and I was young enough to be cheap (cheap and fancy, always a compelling combination). But also, this senior-level woman had just given me the equivalent of TSA Precheck on my career.

I started as a producer for Washingtonpost.com one week later, dedicated to creating content for a partnership with Encyclopedia Britannica.

WHEN OPPORTUNITY KNOCKS...

I want to pause here to point out that I understand the level of privilege this story reveals. My credentials likely influenced Jude's desire to meet with me, and my upper-middle-class upbringing undoubtedly gave me confidence and ease in that newsroom. Yes — and, all the fancy degrees in the world wouldn't have mattered if I hadn't reached out to Jude in the first place. No one came knocking on my apartment door to say, "Hey, we heard you went to an Ivy League school and are looking for a chance to be creative and leverage your communication skills — here is a silver platter full of jobs that might interest you." I had to make active choices in pursuit of what I wanted. Still, I know that we don't live in a meritocracy where all moxie is received equally; not to mention, sometimes, luck is a factor. I imagine that no matter who you are, the following lessons might apply:

1) Pay attention to what feels like "yes." Jude's resume felt like "yes." Follow the "yes."

2) It never hurts to ask for what you want, like when I emailed Jude — someone senior in her field — and asked for a coffee date. Seriously: When you assume the answer is "no," and don't ask, you make it a definite "no," eliminating even a one percent chance that the answer might be "yes." Don't negotiate against yourself.

3) Bring thoughtfulness to your interactions with people. I didn't just write to Jude and say, "Hey, I'm looking for a job, can we meet?" I took the time to articulate what it was about her experience that spoke to me and invited her out for coffee. Thoughtfulness and personal touch matter.

Addendum: If you write a thoughtful email to someone and never hear back, it doesn't mean that you suck, or that thoughtful emails are a waste of time; it means...that you didn't hear back. Period. You can imagine a hundred reasons for this, but they're all just that: works of imagination, aka thoughts. Make your best effort, which may include following up once or twice, and then let it go. What happens next is not for you to control. That said, if you really want to work for a particular organization, and you don't hear back from one person, I suggest looking up other people who work there on LinkedIn; see if anyone stands out as someone with whom you're likely to vibe, and if so, try sending them a note (rinse, repeat).

4) When opportunity presents itself, be ready to say "yes, and" — to ride the wave. If, on the elevator ride up from the lobby, I'd said, "Oh, I'm not a coder *or* a content producer," this story might have had a very different ending. Sure, Jude might have coached me a bit to embrace the producer moniker — but, just as likely, she might have said, "Oh, OK," and just shown me the newsroom without making any introductions.

5) Don't lie (duh), but also, don't shy away from generous descriptions of who you are and what you're capable of; we're far too quick to embrace critical descriptions of ourselves as true, and generous descriptions as false. Had I worked previously as a content producer? Yes, but barely. Did I have 10 examples on my resume of companies that had hired me to produce content? I did not. And they'd know that, once I shared my resume, and once they spoke to me. But in that moment, embracing the generous description of myself as a content producer meant saying "yes, and" to opportunity, rather than rejecting it.

SURFING MY WAY TO PURPOSE

My time at Washingtonpost.com ended up being brief, as contracting delays between media partners left me with very little to do. But having this experience on my resume made me appear interesting to the managing editor of PBS.org, who was looking for an editor of news and documentaries. I knew this because a colleague from the ill-fated healthcare think tank had gone on to work at PBS and recommended me for the role. I was surfing life, to once again quote Amy Poehler; I was riding the waves that came my way — improvising — instead of pursuing some kind of rigid, preset plan.

And it was getting me closer to the thing — a thing, at least — that I wanted to do. At PBS, I found deep satisfaction. Not only did I get to help documentary filmmakers translate their stories to the web in creative ways, but also, I got to be part of delivering on the PBS mission: educating and engaging the American public. On my first day there, I felt something different in the air, and I soon realized it was the staff's earnest devotion to a shared sense of service. It was palpable, and it let me exhale. I was meant for mission-driven work, for work with a "why" that satisfied me. From where I sit today, I can trace a connection between the "yes" I felt at this moment, and the "yes" of designing that course at Penn — creating content that helps other people felt, and feels, *right*.

From that point forward, every choice I made in my career was about aligning the purpose of the work I was doing with my own inner sense of purpose. That compass took me from leading content development for PBS, to going out on my own to advise other non-profits and indie media companies on their content and online storytelling, to honing my focus to telling stories online for women and women's organizations...to helping change makers and creative souls raise their voices and tell their stories in powerful ways. The core of the work I did stayed the same, while the details shifted. It turns out, while storytelling may be the main thing I want to do, remaining open to shifts and pivots, being ready to improvise, has been essential to my satisfaction.

From that point forward, every choice I made in my career was about aligning the purpose of the work I was doing with my own inner sense of purpose.

In the end, I think Conan's message was close to accurate, but unfortunately perpetuates the script that there is one right choice out there for all of us — one "thing" we want to do. The truth is, the most fulfilled adults I know never stop being open to discovering the things, plural, that they want, both as part of their paid work and beyond it; I'll talk more about this in the next chapter.

A couple of years into my time at PBS, I was leading a workshop about how to tell your film's story online for a group of independent producers at WGBH in Boston. At lunch, one of the participants came over to me and said, "So, how about you? Are you a producer?"

I was gobsmacked: Me? A producer? No way.

"Oh, no," I told her.

It strikes me now that this answer was in direct opposition to my "sure, I'm a content producer" response in the elevator with Jude. I think that the work I did with award-winning filmmakers shifted my sense of what it meant to produce something, and made me feel less like a creator, more like someone who helped other people create things.

"Huh," she said, looking at me — really looking at me. "You seem like someone with stories to tell."

I *was* someone with stories to tell. And I still am. I have never stopped writing — sometimes more, sometimes less; sometimes published by someone else, sometimes for my own website, blog or newsletter. I've self-published two books (counting this one), finished several scripts for original TV pilots (one even advanced to the finals in a

Sundance competition, which makes me so proud), blogged for years, published essays and humor pieces and articles offering professional guidance. Over the years, I figured out that the more I told my own stories, the better I got at helping other people tell theirs — and vice versa. To this day, I am grateful to that filmmaker (whose name I wish I could remember) for reminding me: *Oh yeah; I'm someone who makes things.*

Thinking back on that ridiculous interview at the healthcare company, so many years ago: Would I advise an unborn child to be born today, or 2,000 years ago? What a crock. It's not the unborn child that needs guidance; it's the in-the-flesh young person. They — you — need to hear stories of how we've carved our paths in this world, so you can feel more supported as you carve your own path forward and do the things you want to do, shaping the world the way you want it to be shaped.

You need to learn to improvise, with confidence.

YES, NO, MAYBE

I hope one thing you take away from my story is that carving your own path, improvising adulthood, is not about getting every choice you make right, every time. It's about continuing to try. I ended college on such a high note and started my post-college life on such a low one. But that wasn't the end. I kept making choices.

You can always keep making choices. And, in fact, you must. You're part of the show, remember, not just an audience member.

Improvising adulthood is not about getting every choice you make right, every time. It's about continuing to try.

In our late 20s, Jordan and I attended SXSW for maybe the fourth year in a row. If you haven't heard of it, SXSW ("South by Southwest") is an annual festival and conference in Austin, Texas with program tracks dedicated to music, film, and interactive media. I was freelancing now (as was Jordan), but we'd started going yearly back when I worked at PBS, and it became an annual tradition. We loved the vibe — this was before global corporations started hosting branded food trucks, back when most people there made art and code in their garages, and being there to represent PBS made me feel like "the man." But we always felt frustrated by the low quality of the speakers; they were subject matter experts, but they didn't seem prepared to present to a crowd. "We could do better than that," we thought, and then we literally brainstormed what topics we knew enough about to warrant space on the SXSW stage. Number one on our list was freelancing; number two was improv. "What if we shared improv lessons for freelancers?", one of us thought; after all, freelancers, like improvisors, often had to be flexible in the face of the unexpected. We submitted the session, it was accepted, and we were ultimately voted audience favorites.

We came back to the festival twice more, once with "Improv for Everyone," and once with "Change Happens: Improv for an Unpredictable World" (and this was back in 2012, before the world turned up the dial on "unpredictable" to its highest point in my lifetime). Someone who attended one of our sessions approached us about coming to speak to her company, so we briefly spun up a business called Think Improv that offered trainings that brought improv's lessons to the workplace. Jordan wanted to keep going, but at the time, improv was getting so much coverage in the business press, and so many companies were offering trainings on how to "yes, and" your team to success, that it turned me off from leaning into this kind of work full-time.

That might sound counter-intuitive: Everyone's talking about it, so you *don't* want to cash in? I think I wasn't clear on what we had to say that was different. It felt like we were jumping on a bandwagon, even though we weren't. I think leaning into Think Improv full-time also bumped up against my sense of who I was. After leaving PBS and going freelance, I'd launched my first business, Good Things Consulting, helping nonprofits and other clients who were doing good in the world to increase their reach and impact by telling their stories in strategic ways online. This was what I did for a living, not teaching people how to apply improv to their lives.

Irony alert! While I may not have wanted to spend my life teaching people about improv, it turns out I felt a deep passion about sharing its teachings with, well...you (not to mention, Jordan is now a coach and trainer who draws heavily on improv's lessons in his work with leaders). It also turns out, something that feels like a "no" at one point in your life can turn into a big, fat "yes." Your job is to let it — to avoid trying to construct a rigid, linear narrative that makes sense to the outside world, and to instead to make choices that feel like "yes" inside you, where it matters most.

> **Avoid trying to construct a rigid, linear narrative that makes sense to the outside world; instead, make choices that feel like "yes" inside you, where it matters most.**

And remember: no matter what other people or your own anxiety or perfectionism tells you, *you don't have to get it all right, all at once*; what's more, you don't need to think about "getting it right" at all; you just have to — *get to* — make one choice at a time. And your job, as you make each choice, is to pay attention to what feels true, not what is smart or clever or "right."

Before you know it, you're creating a life, instead of just letting life happen to you. And you're discovering not one, big, shiny thing you want to do, forever, but a series of things you want to do, for now... until you don't.

REFLECT

Consider a decision you're trying to make in your life, and play "new choice" with yourself. "What's 'new choice'?" you ask? Surprise, surprise: It's an improv game. Here's an illustration of how it works: Two people improvise a scene, and let's say, at one point, Character A starts eating a piece of cake. Someone on the sidelines calls out, "New choice!" and now, instead of eating the piece of cake, Character A is throwing a piece of cake at Character B. "New choice!" Now Character A is eating the cake, but it has peanuts, and she's allergic. Or she's finding a worm in the cake. Or she's feeding the cake to her dog. Or there is no cake.

I want you to brainstorm five "new choices" you could make as you improvise your way through the decision you're making. Jot down whatever pops into your mind, no judgment. Now write down five more choices, *and then five more*, no matter how absurd they might seem. For example, if you're trying to decide whether to quit your job, you might write down:

1) Quit tomorrow

2) Quit in one year, and spend the next year job searching

3) Quit as soon as I get that raise I've been waiting for

4) Have my best friend quit for me

5) Have my dog quit for me

6) Instead of quitting, talk to HR about my issues with my boss

7) Apply for jobs in other departments

8) Hire a career coach to help me figure out what I really want

9) Go work at a bakery like I've always dreamed; use this time to figure out what's next

10) Set up informational interviews with people whose jobs seem cool to me

11) Join the circus

12) Join Teach for America

13) Run for office

14) Hide under the covers and never come out

15) Eat a lot of ice cream

The ideas you generate may all feel like ridiculous nonsense, but bringing this playful, spacious energy to your decision-making process will help you remember that no choice is our last choice (until, of course, it is). And silliness may just lead you to your truth. After all, as the Greek philosopher Heraclitus once wrote, "Man is most nearly himself when he achieves the seriousness of a child at play." I'll go out on a limb and say this truth transcends gender, so even if you aren't a dude...take heart.

In my case, as much as I loved my work at PBS, I realized that, unfortunately, finding meaningful work wasn't a panacea; my job meant a lot to me, but I still felt restless, like there was something missing. We act as if getting the right answer to the question, "What do you want to be when you grow up?" will solve all our troubles, but I was realizing that my job title wasn't going to be the whole story of my adult life.

SCENE 4

EXPLORE LIFE BEYOND WORK

"Do whatever brings you to life, then.
Follow your own fascinations,
obsessions, and compulsions.
Trust them."

- Author Elizabeth Gilbert

Back to our imaginary improv theater: It's a new night, and a new audience files in. Backstage, the performers warm up, getting ready to take the stage. One of them is Rudy, a newer improvisor who's been down themselves lately. They know they're spending too much time on the sidelines second-guessing their instincts and putting the burden on their castmates to carry the show. "Tonight," they tell themselves, "I'm joining the first scene, no matter what."

The lights go up, the music starts, and the performers run on stage. Jaclyn, whom everyone can always rely on to make things happen, introduces the group and asks the audience for a word of suggestion. "Feathers!" someone cries out. "Thank you," Jaclyn says, and crouches down center stage, her posture tense, her eyes on a distant horizon. "That falcon better come back to me," she says, as the other actors file offstage — all of them except Rudy.

"He's a good li'l falcon," Rudy says. "Better than that panda of yours. He'll come back."

A deathly silence. Then: "You got a problem with my panda?"

"Yeah, I've got a big problem with your panda," Rudy replies. "That panda owes me 7,000 bucks."

The scene continues from there. Later, at the bar next door where people hang out after shows, someone compliments Rudy on how funny the panda scene was. Rudy finds themselves thinking: "If I hadn't decided to be in that scene, I wouldn't have been there to receive Jaclyn's opening line. If I hadn't yes, and-ed her line about the falcon, I wouldn't have mentioned a panda — who knows where that idea came from, it just popped into my head! And I certainly never would have come up with the idea of a freeloader panda who owes me money."

Action begets action. Choices lead to discovery, which leads to more choices. And all of it passes us by if we're stuck in the wings, thinking about what we'll do next.

A WHOLE NEW WORLD

By my mid-20s, I'd improvised my way into work I found fulfilling, and yet somehow, I found myself feeling deeply unfulfilled.

As editorial director of PBS.org, I had a job whose mission I loved, immersed in architecting stories that mattered to me with people I admired. But I was also stressed out big-time from office politics, and I was still filled with this driving sense that things were incomplete. Turns out, that's how a lot of creative people feel when they aren't doing enough of their own creative work. But I'm getting ahead of myself.

Jordan and I had been putting money away for a vacation, and after a little research, we decided to travel to Costa Rica. The photos of rainforests and beaches depicted a kind of natural beauty that seemed unreal; the idea of experiencing these places for myself felt thrilling. I loved that the country had more teachers than police officers, and that we could stay in places that seemed sincerely committed to minimizing their environmental impact, while channeling revenue back into the local economy. Plus, our budget would go further there than some of the other places we considered.

We arrived late at night and got a cab that sped through the darkness to the inn where we'd be staying, which was located on a coffee farm. All we could see were lights twinkling in the valley below. The next morning, we opened our curtains and saw green everywhere. As we explored the lush grounds, the bright, delicate scent from the orange trees mixed with the aroma of strong coffee coming from the inn's open-air restaurant. I felt a sense of presence and connection that I hadn't felt in ages — or maybe ever. Later in the week, we traveled to Manuel Antonio State Park on the Pacific coast, where we hiked in a rainforest, swam at the base of a waterfall, and read books while lying in hammocks. It was heaven.

I felt a sense of presence and connection that I hadn't felt in ages — or maybe ever.

There's a saying in Costa Rica: "Pura vida," or "Pure life." Between the lush biodiversity teeming all around us and the incredibly friendly people we met everywhere we went, I felt connected to "pure life," indeed.

Our flight home to DC routed through New York's JFK airport, and the view of the runway through the plane window was so gray and dreary and ugly. How rudely this contrasted with the unyielding color of Costa Rica. As I resumed my daily life, I noticed the beigeness of every building. Why would we choose beige, for our creations, when we could choose a bright, cheerful yellow, green, or blue?

I craved reconnection with the essence of life that I'd felt on our trip. I saw a flyer advertising a yoga class, and something inside me pinged: *Pura vida.* In other words: I felt a "yes."

ONE THING LEADS TO ANOTHER

The first yoga class I ever attended was held in a local church. When I got there, I found out it was cash only; I had no cash, so back on my snow boots went, and I ventured out across icy sidewalks to find an ATM. Then I hustled back to the church (to the extent that you can hustle while trying not to fall on your butt) where I paid and was able to join the class in progress.

I found an open spot in the crowded room and began copying the movements of the people around me. It was as if I'd been dropped into a group of dancers who'd been rehearsing together for weeks; the choreography was like a foreign language whose sounds I could mimic, poorly, without any sense of their meaning. I stuck out my arm, I bent my leg, and I waited for enlightenment.

As someone who now has been practicing yoga for over 20 years, picturing the hour I spent aping the people around me feels like watching a "Saturday Night Live" sketch. Needless to say, when the end of class came, I did not feel one with life — and yet, something told me that if I could learn the movements, this might just be something I'd love. Plus, they served tea and cookies at the end. Score.

Soon after my ridiculous first attempt at yoga, the woman who ran the class, Kimberly Wilson, opened her very own studio in a narrow brick building just off Dupont Circle. Called Tranquil Space, it became the place where I learned how to actually do this yoga thing. I signed up for a "Newbie" series and learned about yogic breath and the six basic movements of the spine. It felt sort of absurd — wait, why do I feel so different when I think about breathing from my belly? doesn't my breath start in my lungs? — but the good, buzzy feeling in my body at the end of class kept me coming back.

Then one day, in the changing room, I saw a flier for a workshop series that the studio was offering for women artists. We would read something called *The Artist's Way*, and meet weekly to — well, I wasn't exactly sure, something about recovering our creativity? It spoke to me. I decided to sign up.

I want to pause for a minute here and point out that if I hadn't stepped outside of my normal routine and traveled to Costa Rica, I may not have felt the spark that led me to try yoga — which in turn might have meant that I never heard about this workshop series, which, spoiler alert, changed my life. As did yoga, as has every single step along my path, but — reading *The Artist's Way* is one of those "before" and "after" moments for me: There's life before I read it, and life after.

If you aren't familiar, *The Artist's Way* is a book that asserts everyone is an artist, creativity is a spiritual force, and we are healthier and happier when we access our repressed creative spirit and invite it out to play. I'll never forget the experience of reading the book's introduction. Jordan and I were driving back into town after a weekend away with friends. The author, Julia Cameron, started off talking about the sacredness of creativity, and she referenced God, while acknowledging that some readers might not feel comfortable with that idea; for us, she recommended substituting "the universe." My hackles went up: Was this some sort of weird religious book? Was the author a kook? (My more open-minded current self is not proud of those reactions, but it's how I felt at the time.)

Those concerns quickly melted away, though, as sentence after sentence, Cameron held a mirror up to my own inner life. I remember gasping and saying to Jordan, "You've gotta hear this," as I read line after line that spoke to me on a level deeper than any other book ever had. It was like she saw some part of me that no one else had ever seen before, me included. Let's call it my creative soul.

I would proceed to have a series of "holy shit" moments as I worked through the book. A chapter might begin, "At this point in your journey of recovering your creative self, you're likely feeling angry," and I'd be like, "I *am* angry! How did you know?!" It was... weird. And powerful. I dug up so many old origin stories about why I wasn't allowed to pursue my creative passions — stories about money and acceptability and worth. I named the fears that stood in my way.

It was cathartic AF. Soon after I finished *The Artist's Way*, I launched my first blog, "Multitudes," inspired by the Walt Whitman quote: "Do I contradict myself? Very well, then, I contradict myself. I am large; I contain multitudes." It wasn't long until I found improv (number two pencil! the heavens opening!). I was coming home to myself and finding myself at the same time.

So. Much. Yes.

AND...

In some ways, this was a great time of my life. I was having a creative awakening, and I was doing work at PBS that was deeply meaningful to me. What's more, my outer life was coming into greater alignment with my inner life. Kimberly, the woman who ran Tranquil Space, inspired me that such alignment was possible. To behold her life — the way she ran the studio, the book she'd written, even the shop at the studio that she curated with clothing she'd designed — it all felt like a physical expression of the energy and personality that showed up every time she walked into a room. She was the first person I'd ever met who showed me it was possible to design your life in a creative way that expressed your identity.

With so much going right, I must have been in a permanent state of bliss — right?

Wrong.

Office politics drained me. My job included enforcing PBS's guidelines with every producer who contributed content to PBS.org, which meant a lot of battles over things like how big a Flash file could be. I couldn't give a shit about Flash files, but the good girl in me stood at attention like a soldier, devoted to upholding not only the PBS mission but also its timelines and technical specifications. It was not fun. Producers, and likely a few colleagues, called me "Demanda" behind my back. When someone finally told me about this nickname, I made a beeline for my car and drove home crying.

But it wasn't just work stress that was bringing friction to my days. I continued to feel an unceasing dissatisfaction. What's more, I felt *angry* — angry at the Weight Watchers points I was counting (something I shudder to think about, now that I know diets are nonsense), the tight budgeting we were constantly doing, the managing of calendars. I was spending so much time and energy tracking and following rules and plans and not enough time creating to balance it out. One night, when I was especially upset, Jordan said, "C'mon," and he took me on a walk, and then he told me to scream. "Just let it all out," he said. My sweet husband...and those poor neighbors. I screamed. I can't remember if it helped.

I was spending so much time and energy tracking and following rules and plans and not enough time creating to balance it out.

"Do you maybe want to try therapy?" Jordan asked me, and I dismissed the idea. I dismissed it a few times until I finally said, "Fine, I'll go."

THIS IS THE PART WHERE I PLUG THERAPY

Cut to me sitting in a therapist's office and her saying, "It sounds to me like you have anxiety and depression."

Sound of record screeching.

What now?!

Weren't depressed people curled up in the fetal position, unable to get out of bed?

Turns out, not necessarily. Also turns out, not everyone wakes up with a heavy pit in their chest every morning that they need to overcome. That pit had been with me for as long as I could remember. Once I got up and started my day, I could shake it off — or so I thought. All that anger I'd been feeling? That was masking sadness. Deep, deep, sadness. And my constant stress? A lot of that was the churning of my own anxiety run amok.

Today there are pockets of our culture that have normalized mental health challenges and the idea of going to therapy. There are also more depictions of people addressing their mental health in constructive ways in the media and entertainment we consume — just look at how Olympian Simone Biles modeled prioritizing her mental health on the world stage. Granted, mental health stigma is still prevalent, and devastating; I don't mean to suggest that everyone everywhere feels totally cool about the idea that their brain chemistry might be hurting them, or that they might benefit from therapy. But thanks in large part to people sharing their stories online and beyond, I do think it may be less likely today than it was in the early aughts for the idea that you have anxiety or depression to completely sneak up on you.

Either way, there I was, with a diagnosis and a referral to a psychiatrist who could help me find medication that would help. The next year or two were a roller coaster. After giving a particular medication enough time to build up in my system, I'd find that it helped me feel less depressed, only for my anxiety to skyrocket; or a pill would help me for a month or so, maybe longer, and then it would just...stop. And around and around we went. It was an fairly anxiety-producing process, for someone trying to reduce her anxiety.

Finally, I found something that worked for me, that kept working. "There's the Amanda I remember," my mom said, and I struggled with whether the happier Amanda she recognized was authentic or performative. Was my depression more authentic? A lot of people who are diagnosed with a mental illness grapple with these kinds of questions. Over the years, I've come to believe that it's more important to prioritize your ability to feel good navigating the world than to hold on to a more troubled state simply because it may be more "real."

After all, what is "real," anyway? As Jordan once said to me, in our teens, "Reality is subjective." At first, I couldn't even wrap my mind around the idea; now it seems obvious. What I see, smell, taste, hear, feel — it's unique to how I experience the world. Same for you, same for everyone.

UNDERSTANDING OUR WIRING

In my 20s, I'd never heard of the word "neurodivergent," but years later, when I became the mother of a neurodivergent child, I'd learn all about it — the idea that, as author and fellow parent Debbie Reber puts it, we're all "differently wired."

For now, the closest I'd get to understanding neurodiversity was learning about my anxiety and depression. Another pivotal moment for me was reading a book called *The Highly Sensitive Person* by Elaine Arons, PhD. Like my experience with *The Artist's Way*, reading it made me feel like someone had been spying on my insides. Holy hell. Other people felt things this intensely? I'd always thought it was just me. Over the years, I would become more and more aware of how my hyper-sensitivity, not just emotionally but also on a sensory level, affected the choices I made. For example, working in an office was so incredibly draining for me — the noise; the fluorescent lights and stale air; the emotions of so many people swirling around me; the need to be constantly available, and therefore unable to get into a state of deep flow.

> **Over the years, I would become more and more aware of how my hyper-sensitivity, not just emotionally but also on a sensory level, affected the choices I made.**

Then there was the time we were visiting NYC — years before we lived there — and the discount store Century 21 was so crowded, so full of people, so overpoweringly loud from the music and the conversation, that I had to flee across the street to sit on the curb and get my bearings. It's the closest I've ever been to a panic attack. The word "attack" is apt; I felt like my entire self was being assaulted. For other people, presumably, it was just shopping.

THE STORIES WE TELL, AND THE ONES WE DON'T

The powerful effect that both *The Artist's Way* and *The Highly Sensitive Person* had on me represent the power that stories have on our lives, something I was learning so much about at PBS, in the midst of award-winning artists and journalists who devoted their lives to telling stories they felt needed to be told. I had never thought about the idea of representation mattering, or wondered whose stories got told on TV, and whose didn't — or why. I collaborated with independent production companies like the (aptly named) Independent Television Service (ITVS) and American Documentary Inc. and was deeply moved by their commitment to telling stories with and about people whose lives were not, let's say, captured by the latest episode of "Friends."

I was especially inspired by the first-person documentary storytelling that American Documentary Inc.'s "POV" series showcased, and by the idea that people who were typically the subjects of media could instead be the shapers of it — queer people, disabled people, people who grew up in extreme poverty. It's fair to say this moment in my life ignited what would become a lifelong obsession with who gets to tell the stories that shape our world, something that would later lead me to dedicate my life to helping diverse people tell their own stories, in their own authentic voices...and to writing this book.

From Costa Rica, to Kimberly, to this influx of diverse narratives, I was being reminded that the world was vast and my corner of it was small — but exploring, and trying new things, made it bigger. Exploration — choosing to try new things that felt like they might be "yes" — also helped me discover new paths to happiness, from mental health treatment to blogging and the belle of the ball: improv. Improvisors pull details and emotions from the well of their experiences — which means, they need to have experiences! So do we all. Seek out new experiences and people to feed your soul.

And remember to say "yes" to a world beyond your job. Even putting aside the profound ways that improv unlocked me, the simple fact of needing to leave work at a certain time to make it to improv class — or, later, improv practice, and shows — made a huge difference to my wellbeing.

Remember "new choice"? Well, not only does that improv game spark expansive thinking when we're feeling stuck, but also, it can lead us to try things that bring joy into our lives. The next time things feel impossible, remind yourself that discovering something entirely new is just one choice away. Change the channel. Try a hobby or activity you haven't tried before. You never know what your next choice will open up for you.

Here are a few suggestions to get you started:

- Set a five-minute timer and free-write (no editing, no second guessing) in response to this prompt: "It might be fun to..." Now reset the timer, and try this prompt: "If I were six times bolder, I would..."

- Write a list of 3-5 people who you think are interesting, or who seem to be having fun in their lives. They could be people you know, famous people, even fictional characters.

- Keep a media diary for a week. How do different podcasts, shows, books, movies, and music make you feel, emotionally and in your body? Take notes, and then see what patterns you can find, if any, about media that leaves you feeling hopeful or inspired.

As for me, as I explored the world and found new sources of satisfaction, what I still didn't realize was that happiness and fulfillment were not fixed states. You didn't crack the secret code and then land in a permanent place of contentment. I was always changing, and the world around me was always changing. In other words: I was learning that the power to choose isn't the same as the power to control.

And perhaps nothing reinforces your lack of control as much as moving to New York City.

SCENE 5

CHOOSE YOUR PLACES

Izzy's been taking improv classes for a few months at this point, and it's time for her first show. She's nervous and excited as she and her teammates take the stage. Howard, a fellow performer, gets a suggestion from the audience — "pizza" — and they're off to the races.

A tiny cast member named Carla skips onstage. Izzy joins her.

"Mommy, I want pizza," Carla says in a loud, sing-song voice.

"Keep your voice down," Izzy hisses, looking around self-consciously. "This is a church."

Carla stage whispers: "I. WANT. PIZZA." She leans in closer. "And if I don't get it, I just might scream."

"You wouldn't dare," Izzy says.

They stare at each other. Carla opens her mouth; Izzy flinches, but it's a fake-out.

"We'll talk about this later," Izzy says. "Now be a good girl."

Carla begins screaming.

"Fine, you can have pizza," Izzy shouts, then looks around, embarrassed.

Carla is triumphant, a smug look on her face. She won!

"But," Izzy says, "can we please get through your father's funeral first?"

In an improv scene, as in life, location matters. A character's story exists in relation to a place, whether it's Tony Soprano in New Jersey, Leslie Knope in Pawnee, or this mother and daughter at their husband's/father's funeral. If Tony Soprano had lived in Pawnee, "The Sopranos" would have been a very different show! So too do our dynamic interactions with places shape our own stories.

SHOULD WE STAY OR SHOULD WE GO NOW?

Strap in, because deciding where to locate my story — which is to say, my life — has been one of the dominant themes of my adult life. I know how much energy so many of us spend wondering where the "right" place might be, and whether the life we want, or the version of ourselves that we want, would be more attainable elsewhere. I've lived out the answers to those questions, and it's been both painful and deeply rewarding.

Jordan and I always felt like fish out of water (Tonys in Pawnee?!) in Washington, DC. We grew up nearby, and Jordan went to the University of Maryland, only about 30 minutes from the city. He was a year behind me, so when I graduated from Penn, I moved to DC to finally be closer to him. Our plan was to move to San Francisco as soon as he was done with school. We'd spent a week together there, and it felt like a honeymoon. We fell in love with the place, and wanted to experience more of our lives there.

Then we got engaged. Which was amazing! Except that suddenly, every minute I wasn't working was spent planning our wedding. Increasingly, the idea of a cross-country move felt out of reach for two young people without much money. This was before the internet was anything like it is now, so we couldn't easily pore over job or apartment listings or research neighborhoods, the way people planning a big move like this could today. And we couldn't afford to live there without having jobs already lined up. We decided to stay put for the time being.

We were in DC by default, then, and not by choice — except, well, that's not entirely true. We chose to stay, but we hadn't chosen DC for ourselves the way we had chosen San Francisco. It was more about accepting limits than choosing what our hearts wanted most. And sometimes, that'll happen! Life isn't just one big joyride. And making a choice that isn't fully aligned with your heart, or your intuition, doesn't mean you're stuck forever. Because, say it with me now: you can always make another choice.

You can always make another choice.

...Which we did, a few years later, when we again decided to move west, and make our dreams come true. Unfortunately, a loved one had a very strong negative reaction, and, afraid of hurting them, we decided to stay. Another "Sliding Doors" moment: What if we'd gone anyway? But we didn't.

So, we stayed. And the thing is, we ended up building a life we truly loved. We got deeply involved with Washington Improv Theater (WIT), and ended up on a team together, JINX, which became like a second family; more on this in the next chapter. I look back at that time of life with such tenderness and, if I'm honest, longing. Which goes to show, even when you choose something that feels like "no" — which I don't recommend, but which is bound to happen, for one reason or another, over the course of your life — you can still make choices that increase your happiness.

MOVING ON

Still, I struggled, knowing there was a "yes" there that I wasn't choosing — I thought it was about San Francisco, but now I can see that it was actually about what living there represented to me, which was the chance to be surrounded by a creative pulse. This was something I could not find in DC, and not for lack of trying; I even started a blog, Creative DC, to inspire and showcase creative living in our nation's capital. But despite how many artists lived in the area, and how many interesting things happened there, the energy I was craving, the pulse I wanted to feel, simply wasn't there.

At this point, I had left my job at PBS to start my own business, Good Things Consulting. On my first day of self-employment, I sat on my couch with my dog, Cosmo, beside me, and I thought, "Oh — I'm never going back." The economy was strong and so was business. A lot of people were interested in hiring the person who had just overseen content for PBS.org. Jordan was freelancing at this point, too, and at some point, we realized we could both work from anywhere (this was well before working from home was as common as it is today!). After our failed attempts at moving away, we'd hoped a life event — a new job, graduate school — would ultimately take us somewhere else, but we suddenly realized, we were done waiting.

We couldn't ignore what we wanted any longer. I believe we have chemistry not only with people, but also with places, and fundamentally, Jordan's and my chemistry with DC was just...off, just as my chemistry with Penn had been off. By now, San Francisco had become less appealing to us, and Jordan had been dreaming of living in Manhattan ever since he'd visited as a kid; there was no question we'd find a creative pulse *there*. So, we made our plans, and set sail — er, sold our house, hired movers, and drove up the Jersey Turnpike, arriving in our tiny new East Village apartment at 11pm, only to learn that our beloved couch wouldn't fit through the door.

Welcome to New York!

Despite this not-so-warm welcome, I was so happy to be in NYC. Creative energy and independence of spirit were palpable and visible all around us, from the street art to the tiny independent businesses and complete lack of chain stores. We soaked it up. We were thrilled to discover little restaurants and coffee shops that became "our places." We were enchanted, living in our small apartment near Tompkins Square Park, with its exposed brick and a cast of quirky characters as neighbors. Sure, one of the neighbors had a dog that never stopped barking, and another left garbage in the hall; the NYU students who lived upstairs stomped around at all hours, keeping us from sleeping. Sure, the streets emanated a strong scent of *eau de urine*, and every subway stop was a sauna that left us drenched in sweat. But we were having an adventure, the two of us — we'd done it! — and we loved every street fair, every weirdo, every itty-bitty eatery with the tastiest food our tongues had ever tasted.

CREATING HOME, AGAIN

Even as we fell in love with the city, we struggled to stick the landing. After the first wave of the 2008 recession had spared my business, the second knocked me down. In 2010, I found myself out of work for the first time since I'd graduated from college. After a few months, some very junior-level jobs (for junior-level pay) began trickling in, but suffice to say, my income took a huge nosedive. This was ill-timed, to say the least; as you may have heard, NYC is just a wee bit expensive.

I tried to recreate some of the bedrocks of my life in DC, yoga and improv, and found it was much more difficult than I'd expected. The yoga teacher who came highly recommended left me cold. I even signed up for a yoga retreat her studio was hosting in Costa Rica, hoping it would be a great way to deepen relationships and build community. Unfortunately, the "meh" vibe I felt about the teacher back in New York grew into a full-on dislike of her teaching style; it was 100 degrees the whole time; and howler monkeys woke me every morning at 5am. If you've experienced howler monkeys, then you know how disturbing this was; if you haven't, well, they sound like Chewbacca mixed with the most dissonant, noisy heavy metal music you've ever heard.

I missed Tranquil Space — and tranquil space — a lot.

On the improv front, I discovered that the business model for NYC improv theaters is that they don't let you audition for them until you've taken (paid for) all their classes; back in DC, anyone was welcome to audition. So, I signed up for level 1 improv and found my 33-year-old self, who was not the world's best improvisor but had been doing it for five years and performed in festivals around the country, in class with total newcomers, including people as young as 18. That was annoying, but could have been fine, except it became clear that in NYC, studying improv is less a creative outlet and more a steppingstone to a comedy career (kind of like Penn had felt like a steppingstone to a certain kind of job and paycheck, instead of a place to learn). I had wanted to feel a creative pulse all around me, and I was finding it...but I was also experiencing what it's like to live somewhere that is less focused on creativity for creativity's sake than it is on "making it." The mood in classes and shows felt colder than it had in DC, and the improv style more focused on being funny and clever than on creating grounded characters.

IT WASN'T PERFECT, BUT IT WAS OURS

While other friends were having kids and putting down roots, I'd gone from owning a house to renting a tiny apartment; from running a booming business to coming to a professional standstill; and from being part of thriving yoga and improv communities, to struggling to find places in New York to do these activities I loved. On the TV show "The Office" (I'm obsessed), the character of Andy Bernard says, "I wish there was a way to know you were in the good old days, before you've left them." Part of me felt that way, in my life at that time, as I tried and failed to recreate the pillars of my DC life in a new city. And yet, I felt myself living into another, different set of "good old days" at the same time. Sure, things weren't perfect — but they were *ours*.

I've sometimes wondered whether we made the "right" choice, when we moved away — but the wiser part of me knows, that question itself is a trap. There is no "right choice," there is only this choice and then the next one. I do regret the loss of community, and I also know that staying in DC and always wondering what it would have been like to live elsewhere would not have satisfied me. I would not have felt like I was honoring myself or my deep curiosity about what life was like elsewhere, even if it was only a few hours north.

> **There is no "right choice," there is only this choice and then the next one.**

Since graduating from Penn, I've lived in eleven different homes in three different geographic areas (DC, NYC, and New York's Hudson Valley); that means, on average, I've stayed in one place for an average of 2.3 years. Sometimes, self-judgment comes up, and I think, "What's wrong with you? Why can't you just stay in one place? What are you searching for and is it worth all the thousands of dollars you've spent on moving?" Then a kinder voice clears its throat, and says, "Amanda, you chose what was true for you; maybe you wouldn't make all the same choices if you had to do it again, but at least you can look yourself in the eye and say, 'I have been brave. I have done my best to create a life that honors who I truly am.'"

I know so many people who stayed in places or jobs or relationships for *years* after they were done, *years* after they stopped being happy or anywhere near happy. Why? Because they were afraid of change, afraid that the unknown would be worse than the pain of the status quo, afraid that they weren't allowed to want more. This is deeply understandable, and deeply human — but it is not, from what I've seen, a path to joy. Sure, I live with some sadness around the things I've left behind, and I also live with a deep sense of peace that I have been true to who I am. I have chosen from curiosity and love, not fear. Has my life been perfect? No. But it has been, and will continue to be, *mine*.

"BERKELEY SPRINGS OF THE NORTH"

Our years in NYC were wonderful and expansive — and they kicked our ass. I mean, when you look at what you pay in rent relative to what you get, living in the Big Apple is objectively an illogical choice. The longer you stay, the longer you enmesh yourself in the illogic. And you get much in return, in terms of culture and exposure to interesting and diverse people and opportunities (not to mention, amazing food...did I mention the food?). Until those dividends stop filling you up as much as they once did.

Almost as soon as we moved to New York, we started looking for our "Berkeley Springs of the north." Berkeley Springs is a West Virginia town about two hours outside of DC, and for years it was where we went for the weekend when we needed a break from the city. We'd rent a cabin; pack up some books and brown liquor and our beloved dog, Cosmo; and spend a day or two in heaven. I'd narrate the activities of the birds just outside our window ("Oh my gosh! Look at this little guy! Oh! Here comes a friend — nope, he's flying away..."), and Jordan would tease me: "Who needs The Discovery Channel, when you have Amanda?"

From our East Village apartment, some quick research on weekend getaways in nature pointed us to the Hudson River Valley; we began spending the occasional weekend there, and it was pretty much love at first sight. We felt so inspired by the combination of natural beauty, creative pulse (the area is full of artists who tired of, or got priced out of, city life, and moved north), and so much food culture tied to local farms. As time passed, we started dreaming more and more of what it might be like to live there. But we weren't yet done with city life; it called to us — until, after the pandemic, it no longer did.

Today we live in Hyde Park, New York, on the east side of the Hudson River. There are trees out every window, and it is so blissfully quiet. We are still making friends here, and building our lives — finding our people, and rhythms — but the sense of being in the right place is profound. Some friends recently visited from LA and teased us about how often we pointed out cute little markets that we love. There are breweries on farms with art studios attached; the area is just as enchanting to us now as it was when we first discovered it, over a decade ago.

And it's home. For now. Until possibly, some day, when it doesn't feel right anymore, at which point, we'll make a new choice.

REFLECT

- Do you feel chemistry with the place where you currently live? Why or why not?

- Is there a place you're curious about experiencing, either on vacation or by possibly moving there?

- What are 3-5 places where you feel or have felt really good spending time? They might include a coffee shop, a friend's house, a vacation destination — anything. Why do you think they felt so good? What parts of you, or feelings, did they bring to the forefront?

- What are 3-5 places where you feel or have felt "off," like they just aren't a good fit? They might include a school, a town you've lived in, a particular event you attended. Thinking about it now, why do you think they felt "off," or even bad? What parts of you, or feelings, did they bring to the forefront?

Now that we've talked about choosing the places that are a "yes" for you, let's look at choosing people who are a "yes." After all, improv is about making something out of nothing, together; while solo improv shows are possible, they're the exception to the rule, and without scene partners to surprise and support you, you miss out on a whole lot of fun.

SCENE 6
CHOOSE YOUR PEOPLE

"The practice of improvisation (in contrast, say, to that of writing or painting) teaches something that we are hungry to understand: how to be in harmony with one another and how to have fun. We practice improvisation not only to 'express ourselves' but to connect with others in a more immediate way."

- Improv teacher and author Patricia Ryan Madson

Rudy is late to improv practice. He hurriedly locks up his bike in front of the theater, replaying in his mind all the emails he replied to before he left work. Did he get back to Huma in IT? Yes, and he'll follow up with her in the morning.

He enters the building and descends the stairs, lost in thought. "Rudy!!!!" His team spontaneously shouts his name. He grins. There's Jaclyn, finishing up the protein bar she always eats at the top of rehearsal. Frank nods, which is the most enthusiasm he ever expresses, and Jody and Manny smile. Tasha is doing a headstand in the corner and wiggles their

*toes at him in greeting. "Nice of you to stop by," Jaclyn says, smirking;
then, "Ok everyone, let's get started."*

*They circle up and drop quickly into the warm-ups they do each week,
with only the occasional (frequent) interruption for someone to crack a
joke. Later, they run scenes. Tasha has Rudy in hysterics; in another scene,
he and Manny become father and son, and go unexpectedly deep. "Thanks
for that, I wasn't able to get to therapy this week," Manny teases, but after
practice they end up standing on the sidewalk talking about some real-
deal dad stuff for over an hour.*

*Later, as he bikes home, Rudy wonders if he's ever felt such a strong
sense of belonging as he does with this group.*

"I THINK I'D CONNECT WITH JORDAN."

The first time I saw Jordan, in the halls of Rockville's Richard
Montgomery High School, I had this *feeling* about him. As someone
who was nervous around boys I liked, my response to this feeling was
to never approach him but tell all my friends how hot I thought he
was. Later, when he and I had hardly exchanged two sentences, and
I was going to the Homecoming dance with someone else, I wrote in
my journal, "I don't really connect with John. You know who I think
I'd connect with? Jordan Hirsch."

Damn.

Thank you, thank you, to my intuition, for giving me such a clear
"yes" signal about this person who, sure enough, would turn out to be
my soulmate; as of this writing, we've been together for 30 years, and
married for 25 of them. Sure, I also thought he was the best-looking
guy I'd ever seen, so thank you, too, to my adolescent hormones. But
it wasn't just physical attraction; I just *knew*, somehow. Which I realize might make me annoying, or at the very least, unrelatable, because
not many people enter adulthood having already found someone they

know they want to spend the rest of their life with. Not to mention, the idea of having a single soulmate or finding "your person" are both, of course, scripts — stories about how other people think our adult lives are supposed to go. In truth, many people live happily without ever finding romantic love, or they find it with multiple people. It just so happens, in my case, that my soul recognized, very early, that Jordan was for me.

As sure as I was, and am, about Jordan, once I went to Penn, finding my people, beyond Jordan, suddenly became one of the hardest parts of my life.

I've already shared how alienated I felt during college, and as I said, I think there were a few reasons for this: missing Jordan; suffering from clinical depression and anxiety (oh, that); and the earnest existential crisis of a deep-feeling, deep-thinking young person. Whatever the cause, I spent a lot of time during those years feeling like I was sort of floating along the outside of a world where other people were deeply ensconced in their social lives. By sophomore year at Penn, I had several dear friends with whom I remain close to this day. By senior year, I had a group of friends and roommates that comprised my college family of sorts. But I felt, fundamentally, like a loner. This feeling would stay with me for much of my life, and I'd be lying if I said I didn't still feel that way sometimes.

I've had moments in the last 20 years when I was deeply ensconced in community, and these stand out as some of my happiest chapters. The first time was when Jordan and I became part of DC's improv community; the second was after we became parents. I think these examples are telling: Pursuing an activity you love with other people who love it is such a great way to form deep connections, as is finding others who are navigating the same intense life experience you are.

MY IMPROV FAMILY

About a year or so after my "number two pencil" moment, I was taking a ton of improv classes, as was Jordan, through Washington Improv Theater (WIT). My love for improv approached addiction, at times; at the end of every class, when I knew I wouldn't get to do scenes again for another week, I felt not just mildly disappointed, but devastated. So, I was thrilled when Zack, a more experienced improvisor who already performed regularly with WIT, had the idea to form a new group for promising up-and-coming students — a chance for more people to get stage time, while he got experience as a director. Jordan and I were both invited to join.

The group decided to call ourselves JINX. This came after weeks spent agonizing over the decision; there may or may not have been a spreadsheet involved. We meant it as in, "jinx, buy me a Coke," a nod to being so in tune with someone that you say the same thing at the same time, not "jinx" as in "curse"; we were weird, but not weird enough to want to be in a cursed improv group.

But I digress. The hours, weeks, years I spent rehearsing and performing with JINX would become some of the most joyful, creatively fulfilling times of my life. There was Michelle, a Staten Island spitfire who looked like a porcelain doll; every time she opened her mouth, audiences expected her to say something sweet, and boy were they in for a surprise. There was Joe, a cranky engineer and brilliant improvisor, with whom I clashed more than once, but with whom I also created some of the most powerful scenes I was ever in. Aparna had a wry, absurd sense of humor that fueled her standup comedy and punctuated our shows with comedic gems. Honora was a gifted actor who made unexpected choices that kept our shows fresh. Greg excelled at finding the game of the scene and heightening it in reliably fun ways, and Sean brought real emotion to his performances, often saying less than other performers but, when he said something, elevating the comedy big-time. Then there was Jordan, whose strong emotional choices brought so much heart to our shows, and his willingness to say the thing you "shouldn't" say often brought hilarity.

It's hard to evaluate your own performance, but I think my strength as an improvisor was knowing when to end a scene and start another one; timing these choices well both enhanced the comedy or poignancy of the initial scene and contributed to the successful rhythm of our shows. In improv, we call this "editing," which was fitting, since I spent so much of my time at PBS and afterward as an editor; it also occurs to me, as I write this, that leaving Penn and leaving that first healthcare job gave me a stronger sense of when a scene had run its course.

Over the course of JINX's history, there was also Josh, Alice, Carolyn, Rich, Mike, and Jean-François, all beloved contributors. I focus on my other cast mates because we were the core group who traveled to the most festivals together, including the Chicago Improv Festival, twice, where we rented Airbnb's and spent epic weekends wandering the city, bonding, taking in shows together, practicing, and performing.

SO, THIS IS WHAT COMMUNITY FEELS LIKE

If JINX became like a found family — rehearsing and drinking together every week, performing together, traveling, hanging out on the weekends even when we didn't have shows — then other WIT performers, students, and volunteers became like extended family. We'd watch each other perform, take classes together, hang out at bars together, and just generally form a community of insanely creative, smart, fun people where I felt a profound sense of belonging. One year, I took part in a live improvised movie project that WIT was producing; we improvised a film and screened it for an audience one taped scene at a time, running in and out of the theater and into nearby businesses that had given us permission to film on their premises. Most years, members of the community formed into teams for the city-wide 48 Hour film project, where we produced a movie in, you guessed it, 48 hours, from concept to final edit. I was part of a true creative community, from which I derived so much connection and inspiration.

After a few years in our heyday, members of JINX began having kids; then, as I shared in the last chapter, Jordan and I decided to pursue the siren song of life beyond the DC area. I assumed that with so many improv theaters in New York, it would be easy to find a new improv home, and therefore a new improv community, but I didn't count on how different the vibe would be. In DC, the vast majority of improvisors were people who pursued improv as a fun creative outlet and source of community, on top of their careers; but, as I've said, in New York, it felt like most people saw improv as a steppingstone to a career in show business. We struggled to find people it was fun to play with, which really meant, people we vibed with; we made a couple of close friends, but for the most part, we felt adrift. As hard as it was, this was such an important lesson for me in understanding that the magic was never just improv — it was the people with whom we performed; just as in life, the magic isn't just in finding the "right" job, or doing a type of work that matters to you — it's also and especially finding the people with whom you love to do that work.

Or, as Leslie Knope says in the last episode of "Parks and Recreation," "Now go find your team. Get to work. Whatever that work is that you find worth doing. Do it, and find some people to love who'll do it with you." I like to think that Amy Poehler, the actor who played Leslie Knope, and who is one of my improv heroes, had something to do with that line; even if she didn't, that is some serious wisdom, right there.

One way to find your team is to look for people from whom you want to learn. Every time I've done this, I've been glad. Once, in my 20s, when I was thinking of leaving PBS, I interviewed for a job at a communications consulting company that worked with a lot of government clients. I advanced to the final round, and the CEO of the company said something offhand about how important it is to think about the kinds of people you want to surround yourself with all day. And at that moment, I knew I wasn't going to take the job. I knew that, for all its stresses, working at PBS let me interact with documentary filmmakers and other storytellers I deeply admired; these, not politicians, were the teachers I sought.

Jordan and I made some great friends in New York, but we never did create a community to rival the one we had in DC; though, after we became parents, we became part of a community of families tied to a wonderful neighborhood daycare. Accessing my memories of that time feels like gently shaking a snow globe; the music tinkles, and the glittery snow falls like magic dust onto the sweet tableau inside. We were all in such a vulnerable place, so new to the learning curve of parenthood; we'd see each other dropping off our babies and picking them up, and at the little parties that daycare sometimes had; and as our babies turned into toddlers, we'd all meet up on purpose or through serendipity at the same neighborhood playgrounds. Our daughter talked a lot about this one kid, "Ay-ya," who turned out to be Aria; we became really close with her parents, and our families are still close to this day. Every time we're together, I feel a ping of those early years in Brooklyn, just like when I visit Sean or Greg, and feel a ping of our improv heyday in DC. People, I've learned, are like portals — to different times in our lives, and to different versions of who we were, and are.

CONNECTING WITH EACH OTHER... THROUGH SCREENS

In recent years, especially during the pandemic, my main source of new connections was through work. I have met some truly remarkable humans that way — nonprofit leaders, creative entrepreneurs, and so many others who care deeply about this world of ours and have trusted me with the sacred work of helping them to show the world who they are. I'm so grateful that the work I've chosen to do, and the way I've chosen to do it, has brought so many inspiring, interesting people into my life; these relationships enrich the quality of my days, big-time: inspiring me, teaching me, and making me laugh — a *lot*.

But they're all on Zoom screens. Meanwhile, dear friends from childhood and early adulthood live in the DC area; other dear friends and family members live everywhere from Los Angeles to the Netherlands. Thank goodness for Zoom, on the one hand, for softening the edges of geographic distance; but also, it can feel like I'm living in a science fiction movie when so much of my human interaction is through a screen.

We're living through an epidemic of loneliness, according to surgeon general Vivek Murthy[1]. Many of us, me included, spend more time interacting with people digitally than in person. Is connecting online inherently less impactful than doing so face to face? Sociologist, author, and Massachusetts Institute of Technology (MIT) professor Sherry Turkle writes in her book *Alone Together*,

> "We are lonely but fearful of intimacy. Digital connections and the sociable robot may offer the illusion of companionship without the demands of friendship. Our networked life allows us to hide from each other, even as we are tethered to each other. We'd rather text than talk."

Her words resonate with me. In my experience, internet relationships are not enough; in-person relationships and community are essential to our happiness. Not because screens are evil (this is reductionist), or social media is a dumpster fire (it can be, but it's also a

---

[1] https://www.hhs.gov/about/news/2023/05/03/new-surgeon-general-advisory-raises-alarm-about-devastating-impact-epidemic-loneliness-isolation-united-states.html

positive force for change), but because having people around me who love me and inspire me brings an energy into my life that I prefer to live with, than without.

That said, there is no question that the internet can connect us in very powerful ways that enrich our lives. The way I've formed deep connections with clients is just the tip of the iceberg. Think of queer kids living in hostile environments who find community and support through online connection; think of parents of newborns in the NICU who find solace in the wee hours from being part of an online community of parents who've been in their shoes.

Fostering human connection in our complex world is an art. I'm fortunate to know a brilliant connection artist, Mirit Cohen, who started as a client and has become a friend. In her work, Mirit weaves together insights from primatology, Jewish culture, life as a chef, and technology to design meaningful ways of bringing people together. I'm grateful to her and others who spend their lives focused on creating authentic connection, at a time when we're not only officially lonely, but also, in such dire need of discovering that which connects, rather than divides, us.

FINDING THE PEOPLE WHO MAKE YOU COME ALIVE

I believe that we're trying to find the people who are trying to find us. Whatever your feelings about social media or screen time, there's no escaping the fact that as I write this, in 2024, we have access to potential kindred spirits beyond our neighborhood, city, or town. Thanks to technology, we can more easily find people with shared passions and values, people who make us feel inspired and connected and alive, from all over the world. And we need not sit idly by and hope they appear. Instead, we can create an intentional, authentic, consistent online presence — one where we talk about things that truly matter to us, in a voice that is truly our own; when we do, it's like sending up a beacon that like-minded souls can use to find their way to us. This has happened in my own life, and I've seen it happen for my friends and clients, over and over again.

I believe that we're trying to find the people who are trying to find us.

Ever since my JINX days in DC, I've longed for an in-person community, and it's only recently, since moving to the Hudson Valley and enrolling Ali in a democratic school, that I've started to feel the community-shaped hole in my life start to fill in. If DC was a "yes" on the people front, but a "no" as far as place; and NYC was a "yes" for place, and a "yes" for people, but not a "yes" for community...we may finally be experiencing a chapter of our lives where it's "yes" across the board. It's still early days, but — and — I'm hopeful.

As I meet new people at places like back-to-school picnics, I draw on my skills as an improvisor. I pay attention to who feels like a "yes" — who energizes, rather than drains, me. I employ "yes, and" to build on other people's ideas, erecting conversational bridges between their life stories and my own. Learning to improvise, after all, is really about learning how to improvise with other people; none of us exists in a vacuum. Which is why finding people who make you feel safe, relaxed, and free to be your weird and wooly self is one of the most important things you can do.

In an improv show, the best scenes are the ones where laughter comes from a place of truth: "Oh my gosh, I can't believe she just said that, I feel that way all the time" (guffaw). Similarly, in life, the conversations and relationships I value most are the ones where each of us feels relaxed enough to be our authentic selves; inevitably, these are the conversations and relationships that spark the most delight.

The world is full of wonderful potential scene partners who can help you improvise a life of fulfillment and joy; my wish for you is that you find them, both in the physical world, and online.

REFLECT

Here are some questions to consider as you assess the "scene partners" in your life, past, present, and future:

- Who energizes you? Who drains you? Jot down your answers. And choose, in this moment, to spend more time with the people that energize you, and less time with those who are an energy drain.

- What is a specific example of a time that interacting with an individual or a group of people online helped you feel seen, heard, inspired, or otherwise supported? Now, the flip side: What is a specific example of a time that interacting with an individual or group of people online made you feel even more disconnected?

- What is a specific example of time that interacting with an individual or group of people in-person made you feel seen, heard, inspired, or otherwise supported? Now, the flip side: What is a specific example of a time that interacting with an individual or group of people online made you feel even more disconnected?

- How have you been of service to other people online? How did that feel? How have you been of service to other people in-person? How did *that* feel?

At this point, I invite you to notice how much experimenting I've done as I've carved my path in this world. From DC to New York, from PBS to running my own company, I've tried things and followed "yes" as much as possible, even when it didn't make sense to other people. For example, as I shared earlier, the moment Jordan and I chose to finally have our NYC adventure was the same moment that so many of our friends were having kids and really settling down; and then, not too far into our time in New York, we surprised ourselves and decided to pursue our grandest experiment yet: becoming parents. "New choice," indeed!

SCENE 7

KEEP GOING

"Let everything happen to you: beauty and terror.
Just keep going. No feeling is final."

- Poet Maggie Smith

Izzy has graduated from student to performer, and now it's time for her team's first Saturday night show. They've been killing it on weeknights and are buzzing with excitement as the music starts and they run onto the main stage.

A couple of scenes in, Izzy decides to make a bold character choice as a fast-talking con artist. As soon as she starts talking, she feels weird in her skin, like she's doing a bad caricature instead of actually being the character. Carla, her scene partner, is right there, yes-anding her, but Izzy feels embarrassed and stuck in her head. The audience doesn't laugh at all.

Izzy thinks she might die. She wants to crawl into a hole. She hides out in the wings for the next scene, and the next, and the next, shame crawling up her neck and face.

But then something happens. Two of her teammates are doing a scene and Izzy immediately sees how she could heighten the fun by walking on as their boss. She hesitates — maybe she'll just fuck it up. But she feels how their scene is on the brink of fizzling out, and she knows she can help. Before she can stop herself, she strides on stage, says one line, and can feel how right it is.

The crowd laughs, but what Izzy notices most is how good she feels, how connected with her teammates, and how happy she is that she gets to do this thing she loves.

"MAYBE RARELY TURNS INTO NO"

When you arrive at a place of satisfaction in your life, savor and celebrate it, but don't expect permanence. After all, your life is not an improv scene, it's an improv *show* — and shows are composed of many scenes. Sometimes the scene changes because shit happens, and it's up to you to "yes, and" your way to a better outcome; other times, a voice deep inside you yearns for something new — like when I realized that I wanted to become a mom.

I spent most of my adulthood certain that parenthood wasn't for me. Walking down the street, I'd barely notice kids or babies; meanwhile, I'd want to stop to pet every single dog I passed. As far as I could tell, kids screamed a lot, and parents became enslaved to their screamers, losing all other aspects of their identities while cleaning up a whole lot of Cheerios. Why would I want this?! Then, in my early 30s, I held my friend Wendy's newborn son while he slept, and a kind of physical maternal yearning woke up inside of me; it wouldn't go away, no matter how much I willed it to. Still, being a mom didn't jibe with my vision for the creative life I wanted to lead, and Jordan was about zero percent interested, so we fell into a pattern of occasionally discussing the subject before once again putting it aside.

Fast forward to my first appointment with Dr. Rothenberg, the OB/GYN I found after we moved to New York.

"So, do you want to have kids?" she asked.

"Oh, that's a question mark," I said, laughing.

Dr. R looked me in the eye, and she said, "In my experience, 'maybe' never turns into 'no,' and it only gets harder as you get older."

Jordan and I ultimately decided to take the leap — to say "yes, and": Yes, we never thought we wanted a child; yes, we're happy with our lives, and scared that having a kid will change that; *and*, parenthood is calling to us strongly enough that we're gonna go for it. In 2012, our daughter Ali was born. I feel like doing cartwheels and screaming from the rooftops about how amazing she is, and how much I love her, but that's not the point of this book, so I'll spare you! Making the decision to become a mother and exploring all of the profound ways it changed me is a whole book unto itself (literally — if you're curious, check out my first book, *Feeling My Way: Finding Motherhood Without Losing Myself*); for now, suffice to say that if moving to NYC is a crash course in lack of control, motherhood is like that crash course compressed into a tiny pill that hits your bloodstream like a tsunami.

I share these glimpses into my motherhood journey not because I assume every one of you will have or has a child (you do you), but to illustrate the curves and hills and valleys in my life story — the fact that nothing played out the way I had expected, and every time I felt any kind of self-satisfied sense of "having things figured out," I was once again confronted with profound levels of not-knowing. As Ali grew from a baby into a toddler and beyond (she's currently 12 years old, be still my heart), I found myself in a scene I'd never expected; and yet, it was a scene I chose, albeit without fully understanding just what I was choosing, because how can you possibly understand motherhood, or anything new in life, until you're in it?

ZIGGING AND ZAGGING

Sometimes you don't get to choose the transition from one scene of your life to another. Sometimes, circumstances unfold that you never would have chosen. The wise Buddhist monk, Pema Chodron, wrote a book about this that I highly recommend, aptly titled *When Things Fall Apart*. Just as on an improv stage, there is always the distinct possibility that no one will laugh, in life, there is always the possibility that things will go south; in other words, sometimes, we just bomb.

Just as on an improv stage, there is always the distinct possibility that no one will laugh, in life, there is always the possibility that things will go south; in other words, sometimes, we just bomb.

In 2015, six years after we'd moved to NYC, Jordan and I were struggling. Ali was three, and we were quickly realizing that it really does take a village to raise a child (hat tip, Hillary Clinton). Daycare was expensive, and living in Brooklyn was expensive; when our landlord announced he was going to renovate the building and begin charging $1,000 more a month in rent, we knew we needed to find a new place to live — but where? Surveying real estate listings in Brooklyn and other parts of the city left us feeling deflated; you get so very little for what you pay, in NYC, and we had started to resent this constraint, rather than finding it charming or romantic. We were torn between moving to a town we loved in the Hudson Valley, called Beacon — a place we vibed with, hard — and moving back to DC.

Back to DC?!, you might be thinking. *Didn't you write a whole chapter about how DC wasn't your place?* Yes, and points for paying attention! But, as we watched our parents schlep up and down the Jersey Turnpike to come visit their granddaughter, and to help us out when daycare was closed but we still had paid work to do, we started to feel like maybe we were swimming unnecessarily against the tide. Maybe we could move back, we thought, with our eyes wide open, knowing it wasn't "our place," but savoring the benefits of home, and knowing we could travel, back to NYC and far beyond, to get our fix of places whose energy we truly loved.

So, back we went, moving into a rental that our friend Greg and my dad had screened for us, taking us on a tour via FaceTime. Shortly after moving day, we hosted a big get-together at a bar in our old neighborhood, celebrating the beginning of a new chapter that reunited us with so many dear friends and loved ones. As the months went by, we savored spending time with so many people who meant so much to us — but we also increasingly knew that being there again wasn't right. Living in DC still felt like "no," no matter how much the people were a resounding "yes." Again, I strongly believe that we have chemistry with places; some places make us feel inspired and alive, others stultify us; sadly, DC has always been in the "stultified" category.

Still, I think we would have stayed; listened to the "yes" of the people, if not of the place; and made a point of traveling as much as possible. But in the spring of 2016, I got an offer for a full-time job back in NYC. By this point, I was certainly in a better place financially than I had been at my low point in 2010, but my income was still volatile — high one year and low the next in a way that left us overly relying on credit cards to cover the lulls...a dangerous game, to be sure. It had also been ten years since I'd left PBS, ten years that I'd been doing the same kind of consulting, and I felt a crossroads approaching; time for a shift of some sort. I told myself this job offer represented just the shift I'd been looking for. I told myself the work spoke to me, though deep down, I think it was really the money (the salary was *very* appealing), the title (I'd be VP of Content), and the ready-made reason to return to New York. Jordan was instantly on board.

THE WHEELS COME OFF THE BUS

We felt hopeful, on the cusp of a fresh chapter. Since Ali was approaching school age, we scouted Brooklyn neighborhoods whose public schools had good reputations. Almost one year to the day after our move south, we moved back to Brooklyn, saying goodbye to family and to DC friends who likely felt tired of our antics, and hello again to New York friends we'd missed. I started my new job.

Aaaaand, it became clear right away that this was *not* a match made in heaven. Simply put, I didn't fit in. This organization that talked so much about authentic leadership seemed instead to promote conforming to a very particular way of operating. My boss and I thought about content in ways that were diametrically opposed. Everyone in my division sat at a couple of big, communal tables in an open office. For eight or more hours a day, there was no escape from the presence or sounds of other people. For a person who gets over-stimulated by constant noise, and who needs space to do deep work in a state of flow, it was, in a word, hell.

As my work stress grew, it was clear that Ali was struggling, too — a lot. That first summer back in New York, I fielded many a call from camp staff while hiding in the hallway near the office bathrooms, the most private space I could find in our open office. What's more, we'd chosen our new Brooklyn apartment because it was near a school with a great reputation, only to find out that school was overcrowded. The city assigned Ali to a different school, one over a mile away in a neighborhood of Brooklyn with no subway stops, making it difficult to weave dropping her off and picking her up into our daily schedule. But we made it work.

Except, it wasn't really working. Without going into every detail, I'll say it was a very hard period for all three of us. And the hits just kept on coming. It was 2016, and on the morning of Election Day, I took a picture at an intersection in my neighborhood between

President Street and Clinton Street before voting at the library a couple of blocks away. I was so excited. And then, that night, when it became clear that the impossible had happened, I was gutted, and because of my privilege, I was also shocked. I walked into Ali's room, where she was sleeping, and I said, "I'm sorry." My overwhelming feeling in that moment was that if I'd known this was the world I was bringing her into, I wouldn't have brought her here.

A few months later, my boss eliminated my position. He did it in a conversation on Skype, after making idle chit chat about how my weekend had been. I'd never been laid off before — heck, I'd never even gotten a bad performance review. I'd made a big show of closing shop at Good Things Consulting to go in-house. And now I suddenly had no job and no income. Talk about operating without a script.

And yet, in moments like these, when everything seems awful, so many people seem to believe that there is a script — that these circumstances are happening *to* them, and there's nothing they can do about it. *Au contraire!* While I don't mean to downplay how much pain we can experience in this life, much of it far more extreme than anything I've narrated in these pages, what's also true is that we can always make a choice — we can always say, "yes, and."

So that's what I did.

FINDING MY WAY BACK TO "YES"

I started by asking our landlord if he might consider letting us out of our lease early, since I'd lost my job, and we could no longer afford the rent. He turned around and asked us what we would be able to pay, and while he couldn't match our ideal number, he agreed to reduce our monthly payments by several hundred dollars. This is unheard of in New York City, and the experience serves as a reminder to never assume that the answer to what feels like an audacious question is "no." Always ask. Always give people a chance to say "yes."

*Always ask. Always give people
a chance to say "yes."*

My friend Greg, from JINX, was running a writing group at this time, and invited me to join. This creative outlet was just what I needed. I started writing a TV script and remembered just how much dramatic writing lights me up. Since then, I've written several more screenplays, and I still dream of getting to bring them to life; I've submitted to some competitions and making it to the final round of the Sundance Episodic Lab stands out as one of the most thrilling experiences of my life. But after a brief stint in an MFA program, I decided — sitting on a mountaintop in California, in the middle of a weekend trip with other creative moms — that I did not want to pursue a career in TV writing. First, if I was really going for it, it would mean moving my family to LA, which I love, but which is not where I want to live. More essentially, the industry appears brutal, and breaking in seems to require a singularity of focus that I do not wish to summon, given all the other parts of my life and work that I value. As much as I would love to be part of shaping the stories people consume in their binging hours, and contributing to the cultural conversation in that way, for now, I'm content with TV writing as a hobby.

In the meantime, as I contemplated what was next for my career, I knew I had to feel that my work was creating a world I could stand for my daughter to live in. I found myself thinking about one of my favorite clients from before I'd briefly gone in-house. Her name was Pat Mitchell, an amazing media executive and activist and one of my role models; she'd hired me to help her craft her online presence, which included helping her shape the story she wanted to tell about herself and her work. I realized I'd had a few other individual women as clients over the years, in between the nonprofit organizations and socially conscious start-ups, and I loved doing this kind of work with them.

I thought about the violent misogyny of the 2016 election, and of all the white women who'd elected you-know-who despite it. What would it take to give these women the conviction and courage necessary to vote in their own best interests? Still passionate about the power of the stories we tell (and those we don't) to shape our world, I started thinking about the potential for a business focused on helping women take up more space in the world with their stories and ideas. We could flood the internet with our voices, and in so doing, create a culture where the truth and power of women's leadership was fully on display. Maybe, in such a culture, the power and influence of a candidate who was blatantly misogynist, not to mention racist and ableist, would collapse, like the walls of a leaky, inflatable turd.

In August 2017, I launched my new business: Mighty Forces, a women's storytelling company. "Because the world needs women's stories," my tagline declared.

That fall, actress Alyssa Milano used the hashtag #metoo in a tweet, and suddenly, the movement that Tarana Burke had been building for years was in the national spotlight. As women came forward to call out titans of industry like Harvey Weinstein and shared their stories of abuse, women's stories were in the zeitgeist. If our stories of trauma could be so powerful, I wondered, what might happen if we also shared stories of our talents and triumphs?

Mighty Forces was instantly successful. I poured everything I'd learned about building a business and a brand into its launch — lessons learned through years of uneven success with Good Things Consulting and as a freelancer before that. My choices flowed out of me, and women responded. I felt like a phoenix, rising from the ashes.

Meanwhile, Ali was starting to thrive.

Things were looking up.

FINDING MEANING IN HARD TIMES

Remember: Things are never final, until, one day, they are (depending on your spiritual beliefs, even death may not be the end). You can always make a choice. That doesn't mean you'll experience joy and delight at every step of your journey — there will almost certainly be difficult moments, and experiences that threaten to crush your spirit. But those moments are not the end, unless you choose to make them be.

There will almost certainly be difficult moments, and experiences that threaten to crush your spirit. But those moments are not the end, unless you choose to make them be.

What's more, as spiritual teacher and author Eckhart Tolle has observed, "Some changes look negative on the surface, but you will soon realize that space is being created in your life for something new to emerge" (incidentally, I highly recommend his book, *The Power of Now: A Guide to Spiritual Enlightenment*). That's not a promise that if you sit still after a painful experience, unicorns and rainbows will suddenly appear; but it is a wise reminder that often, in hindsight, we can see that experiences that felt unbearable were perhaps opportunities for us to confront something unresolved within ourselves, in ways that better position us to make choices that are true to who we really are. If I hadn't gone through the incredibly stressful experiences I shared earlier in this chapter, for example, I don't know that I would have birthed Mighty Forces, which has become a source of so much deep fulfillment and joy.

Above all else, remember that there is always a path forward — and for me, this path often lies in helping other people. There's plenty of research showing that being of service is good for our mental health. When we struggle, and we all do, it's a chance to learn something and share that lesson with others in a way that eases their path. Does that mean struggling is fun? That we should relish the darkest, most challenging moments of our lives? Of course not. I'm not a psychopath! Suffering sucks. And, when it happens, it is not the end; it's just a shitty scene in a much longer, fuller show. As the artist Morgan Harper Nichols has said, "Tell the story of the mountains you climbed. Your words could become a page in someone else's survival guide."

Or, as V (formerly Eve Ensler) so wisely said at a PBS Annual Meeting I attended back in the day, "We give what we most want to get, and we teach what we most want to learn." Whatever struggle you experience primes you to be of service to someone else going through that same struggle — not that their experience will be identical to yours, necessarily, but you will be able to empathize with them in ways that others can't, which means you can give them the gift of knowing they are not alone. I know so many entrepreneurs, change makers, and creative souls whose entire career purpose is effectively a map to what they wish someone had told them, taught them, done for them, when they were earlier on their path. Case in point: Here I am, writing a book about what I wish someone had told me as I set off into adulthood. And I'm running a business that inspires people to believe their authentic voice matters — exactly the message I need to remember, over and over again, when I start prioritizing encouraging other people's creative expression over channeling my own.

Whatever struggle you experience primes you to be of service to someone else going through that same struggle.

Yes, sometimes we bomb. But I always remember back to my early days in improv, watching more experienced actors perform. Often, their shows were hilarious, but sometimes, they weren't. In those moments, though, rather than thinking, "These guys suck," I always thought, "This is so awesome, and they are so fucking brave." What makes improv electric and compelling isn't that it's consistently and predictably funny — it's that people are willing to try, wholeheartedly, together.

The same is true in life. It's not about "killing it," it's about having the courage to try, and try again.

REFLECT

At this point, I'd love for you to reflect on the following questions:

- How would you describe the scene you're currently in, in your life?

- What are the primary actions your character is taking — or is not taking?

- How is your current scene different from the last one?

- What is something that sucks right now? This could be anything from a social injustice to an annoying coworker or a piece of your shirt tag poking you in the back. Next, consider: what is something that feels good right now? It could be big, like a relationship going well or a meaningful creative or career milestone, or it could be small, like, "This weighted blanket feels nice," or "That tree is pretty.;';/'

- If, as V said, we give what we most want to get, and we teach what we most want to learn: What do you want to give? What do you want to teach? You have permission to get it wrong, or only half-right...no one's grading you. Just write down whatever comes up for you.

For years, I tried to coach myself out of feeling things that hurt, reasoning with myself in my mind, redirecting my attention to what was positive. Because I feel things so incredibly strongly, and because I spent so many years suffering from untreated depression and anxiety, I decided at some point that negative feelings were intolerable; I tried to bulldoze through them. But as I reached midlife, this caught up with me, in the form of chronic migraines and other physical pain; as we'll talk about more in the next chapter, your body remembers things from every scene of your life, no matter how much your brain wishes to erase them.

SCENE 8

BE PRESENT

"If you're in your head then you're not here with me."

- Improv actor and teacher Susan Messing

Rudy's team has been on stage for about 25 minutes, so it's time to move the show towards an ending. Standing in the wings, Rudy quickly plays back in his mind the scenes they've done so far, looking for stories or themes they might want to tie together.

Just as he's thinking, "Oh, I could bring back the barber shop and the space monkeys," Jaclyn takes the stage, and starts reprising her role of jaded teacher from earlier in the show. Rudy feels irritated; he didn't think that was their strongest scene, but now he should probably join her as the overeager principal. But before he can take a step, Tasha's joining Jaclyn, and she's a space monkey who's been sent to detention — which is being supervised by Jaclyn's teacher. They found a way to connect the two stories!

Rudy relaxes, remembering for the zillionth time that when he trusts his teammates, great things happen. Suddenly, he has an instinct, and before he can second-guess himself, he's shuffling onto the stage as the barber, who, it seems, has also gotten detention.

Soon his teammates are joining the scene as other characters from throughout the show, which ends with Jaclyn's jaded teacher finding hope again, thanks to the cast of oddballs she met in detention.

THE POWER OF THE PRESENT MOMENT

One of the most important tools an improvisor has is presence — the ability to be in the present moment, rather than caught up in thoughts about the past or the future. To state the obvious, being present is very, very hard! But the more connected we are to the present, in body and in spirit, the better able we are to gather important information that informs our next choice, and then the next.

The more connected we are to the present, in body and in spirit, the better able we are to gather important information that informs our next choice, and then the next.

Another way to describe being in the present moment is in terms of "embodiment"; as my friend, somatic coach Jay Fields, explains, embodiment is *experiencing* yourself and the world, versus *thinking about* yourself and the world. Easy peasy, lemon squeezy, right? Wrong. Consider all the energy you spend thinking about things: your to-do list, what that person said, what you should say. What if you could shift all that energy and attention into experiencing what's happening to you *right now*? For example, when I tune into the present moment, I notice that my butt is sore on this chair I'm sitting in; my shirt is soft; my dog is sleeping on the carpet nearby, and her chest is rising and falling as she sleeps. These observations might lead me to stand up and stretch, sigh deeply as I savor the feeling of my shirt and lean down to pet my dog. From there, I'd register another set of sensory inputs and make another set of choices.

Noticing that my butt hurts may not sound particularly profound! But once you start tuning into the present moment, it's likely you'll become aware of just how much you've been missing. For example, before I sat down to edit this book today, I couldn't stop thinking about what a big week I had, how tiring it was, or whether I'd meet my editing goal. If I'd let my mind drive, it would have had me relate to the process of editing this book, which is precious to me, as a task to cross off my list, rather than inviting my full presence to the creative process. Aware of how tangled up in my mind I was feeling, I decided to journal and meditate as a way of feeling more embodied; believe me, there are plenty of times when my gut tells me that journaling or meditating will make me feel better, and I don't listen — but this time, I did. While meditating, I noticed pain in my body and decided to practice a few minutes of yoga to work out the kinks and get my energy flowing in a more expansive way. Only after all of that did I sit down to write, and I could feel in my body that I'd activated a fuller presence than the harried Amanda of 40 minutes ago.

You won't always have time for 40 minutes of getting yourself right. In those cases, taking some deep breaths and taking a quick inventory of what you see, feel, hear, taste, and smell, can make a profound difference to how present you are.

On an improv stage, being present might make you notice: *My scene partner just smirked. Deb looks like she has something to say. It feels like time to edit the scene.* Instead of thinking, "Is the audience liking this? How did I end up in a scene about cupcakes, this is lame. What should I say next?", being present might lead me to feel offended at the smirk, and let it drive the sassy tone of voice I use as I say my next line; or to register my offense with a facial expression, giving Deb space to speak; or to end the scene, and start a new one. In each case, I would be advancing the show based on responses that came from being embodied — from experiencing the scene, rather than thinking about it.

If this all sounds hard: Yes, you are correct! After all, we live in a capitalist, information-driven culture that prizes the mind and its capabilities over anything like presence or embodiment; when the body gets attention, it's treated as a problem to be solved: improve your abs, eradicate your eczema, conquer your chronic pain. Our culture also celebrates results (an A! a pay raise! going viral!) over experience (feeling curious! feeling proud! feeling inspired!), so turning your attention to your experience of life can be extremely challenging. But that doesn't mean it's impossible.

THE STORIES OUR BODIES HOLD

I was in my latest decade, my 40s, when I embarked on a journey to become more embodied. It was 2021. Everyone I knew was getting vaccinated and beginning to emerge, masked, from the isolation of covid lockdown — blinking in the light as we tried to figure out what the world would look like, now. I was suffering from migraines half the days of the month — debilitating headaches that sent me to bed in a dark room. Not ideal for parenting a child through a pandemic, or running a business, or, well, anything, really.

In an effort to help relieve my pain, I got a massage at a wellness center in my Brooklyn neighborhood. As I opened up a bit to my massage therapist about my migraines, she told me about another treatment the center offered, something called "somatic experiencing." I'd never heard of it before, but as I read about it later on their website, I became intrigued; the idea was that we hold stories in our bodies, and here was a therapy designed to help us process and release those stories. As someone whose life and work centered around storytelling, this notion resonated. Plus, as traditional doctors failed to identify the source of my migraines, I was increasingly open to different approaches. In addition, I had recently read *The Body Keeps the Score* by psychiatrist and trauma researcher Bessel A. van der Kolk; in it, he makes it clear that our bodies contain information, and store emotions and pain:

"Being frightened means that you live in a body that is always on guard. Angry people live in angry bodies. The bodies of child-abuse victims are tense and defensive until they find a way to relax and feel safe. In order to change, people need to become aware of their sensations and the way that their bodies interact with the world around them. Physical self-awareness is the first step in releasing the tyranny of the past.

In my practice I begin the process by helping my patients to first notice and then describe the feelings in their bodies — not emotions such as anger or anxiety or fear but the physical sensations beneath the emotions: pressure, heat, muscular tension, tingling, caving in, feeling hollow, and so on. I also work on identifying the sensations associated with relaxation or pleasure. I help them become aware of their breath, their gestures and movements..."

In my first somatic experiencing session, my therapist and the owner of the wellness center, Dawn Philips, explained what to expect. First, we'd sit and talk a bit about the things that were on my mind, anything I knew I wanted help with. Then I'd lie on the massage table, fully clothed, and she would place her hands on different parts of my body. Images or feelings might arise; if this happened, she invited me to share them with her.

So, we talked, and I climbed onto the table, and she put her hands on my feet, and all of a sudden, I saw my dad.

I know it might sound absurd. My dad wasn't even on my (conscious) mind that day, nor was he at all related to the things I had talked about at the top of our session. I have a positive and pleasantly uneventful relationship with him, so it's not like, "Oh, of course Dad would show up, it's always about Dad." It is not! But there he was, unsummoned. I continued to have images appear to me throughout that first session, and emerged stunned by how much could be going on in my body without my knowing it. I started seeing Dawn weekly. My migraines didn't evaporate. But I could feel that I was learning a new way of relating to myself and of being in the world. A new form of body awareness had woken up and was here to stay.

When I moved away from Brooklyn, I was lucky enough to cross paths with another powerful healer, Eliza Volk, who has been supporting me with somatic experiencing therapy for a couple of years now. Through her patient and profoundly intuitive coaching, I've learned to really slow down and feel what's in my body — not "I feel stressed," but "My shoulders feel tight," or even, "I feel a kind of clenching energy in my heart." These baby steps of observation end up making a profound difference. When I notice something, it's like it gives the sensation freedom to morph or move. I'll watch as a feeling of clenching in a part of my body transforms into more of a feeling of spaciousness and spreading.

NOTICING "YES" AND "NO"

As I write this, I am so much more embodied than I ever was before. I am more attuned, these days, to whether I need to move or to rest, to venture into the world or savor being solitary. I meditate nearly daily. Being in relationship with myself in this way has dramatically minimized the time it takes me to know whether something feels like "yes" in my body, or "no," and to act on this information. In particular, I find I'm becoming less judgmental of myself when something registers as a "no" that I think should be a "yes." I allow the feeling, and take it seriously, even when I don't understand it. This has been a huge breakthrough: Accepting that I will not always understand my feelings with my thinking mind, but that they are still real and valid and deserving of my attention.

When something registers as a "no" that I think should be a "yes." I allow the feeling, and take it seriously, even when I don't understand it.

What does it feel like in *your* body, when something is a "yes" for you? For me, more than anything, it's a feeling of spaciousness around my heart.

What does it feel like when something is a "no"? For me, it's a heaviness and a kind of clenching energy in my heart and belly.

Throughout this book, I've talked about your power to choose and choose again. The more you connect with your body — and, if it speaks to you, your spirit — the easier it becomes to know what choice you want to make next.

Case in point: Earlier this year, after doing some work with Eliza, I was meditating when a vision popped into my head. I realize that might sound strange, but maybe if you meditate or attend sound baths or do anything along these lines, you've had similar experiences. Anyway, there I was, lying on the bed in my guest room/home office, when suddenly, I saw myself walking in the woods with a trans child, born in a male body, now identifying as female; she had short, asymmetrical brown hair, and she was holding my hand, and she told me, "You're getting it, Mom."

And suddenly, I realized that Mighty Forces was not just for women anymore. I didn't want to be part of making anyone feel excluded. I would serve change makers and creative souls of all gender identities. This isn't to say that other people are wrong to offer services designed explicitly for women; it's only to say that for me, that suddenly felt like tying myself to an old world order.

So, I made a choice.

BEING IN IT, TOGETHER

I opened this chapter with a quote from an improvisor I admire, Susan Messing: "If you're in your head then you're not here with me." When we don't put in the work to connect to our bodies, and to be present, not only do we cut ourselves off from information that can serve us, but also, we cut ourselves off from other people, because *we aren't there* — we're in our heads.

Like improv, life itself is inherently collaborative. We need to learn how to work with other people, be with other people, love other people, not only to get our most basic physical needs met (food to eat, shelter from the elements) but also for our emotional and spiritual wellbeing. Remember the loneliness epidemic I mentioned in an earlier chapter? Living in our heads isolates us. It also makes it so much easier to see life as something happening to us, not with us — to see ourselves as audience members, rather than performers.

Like improv, life itself is inherently collaborative.

It's easy to be in the audience. If you went to an improv show with the goal of analyzing what you were seeing, you'd start to see all the times one player didn't "yes, and" another, or all the times one character mimed that the kitchen table was center stage when another acted as though it were stage right. You might even spot missed opportunities for jokes or notice flaws in the actors' performances; maybe you'd know for a fact that their Texan accent *sucked*.

Well, no matter how astute the criticism, I will never be as impressed with or inspired by the person judging from the sidelines as I am with the person who dares to perform. As Teddy Roosevelt famously said, and Brené Brown more recently and famously quoted,

"It is not the critic who counts; not the man who points out how the strong man stumbles, or where the doer of deeds could have done them better. The credit belongs to the man who is actually in the arena, whose face is marred by dust and sweat and blood; who strives valiantly; who errs, who comes short again and again, because there is no effort without error and shortcoming; but who does actually strive to do the deeds; who knows great enthusiasms, the great devotions; who spends himself in a worthy cause; who at the best knows in the end the triumph of high achievement, and who at the worst, if he fails, at least fails while daring greatly, so that his place shall never be with those cold and timid souls who neither know victory nor defeat."

As you navigate adulthood, please, be a person who is in the arena. Do not succumb to the false safety of sitting on the sidelines. As Amy Poehler has said,

"I want to be around people that do things. I don't want to be around people anymore that judge or talk about what people do. I want to be around people that dream and support and do things."

You can't create a meaningful existence by sitting in your apartment analyzing your life to death; believe me, I've tried. No amount of smarts or analytical ability will get you from here to there. But you know what will? Dreaming and doing. Trusting yourself to be in the scene and allowing it to unfold.

I am still unfolding, and so are you. Just as in an improv show, you can't know what the final scene will be when you're in the first scene. I never would have predicted each beat of my life story; and yet, in the rearview mirror of midlife, they seem so interconnected and necessary. You cannot predict the future or what Future You will want or need, so focus on connecting deeply and in an embodied way to the present and being in integrity with yourself as you make one choice at a time. If you try to plan it all out, it takes you out of the present moment, which ultimately is all there is. The person who stands in the wings planning the perfect move misses the show.

Don't miss the show. It's your show. It's your life.

REFLECT

I invite you to experiment with something called body scanning, which I'll describe below. I say "experiment" to emphasize that I am not asking you to commit to doing this for the rest of your life; you are not adding yet another "to do" item to your list forever and ever. You are simply committing to trying this at least once and noticing how it feels!

1) Choose a safe place where you feel comfortable closing your eyes for up to 10 minutes.

2) Make yourself comfortable. You can sit or lie down, whatever feels best. Notice how you feel. If 1 is "meh" and 5 is "whoo hoo!" choose a number that represents how you currently feel.

3) Close your eyes and bring attention to your scalp. Now notice your left ear, and your right ear. Your forehead. Your eyebrows. The space between your eyebrows. Your nose. Your cheeks. Your jaw. Notice how your whole head feels. Now notice your neck. Proceed like this until you've made it down to your toes. (Apps like Insight Timer and Headspace have audio you can listen to for free that will guide you

through a body scan so you can just relax into it and not have to guide yourself.)

4) Notice, again, how you feel, on a scale of 1-5. Did your number go up at all?

It takes courage to improvise. Then again, it takes courage to be part of any show, and let's be real, it takes courage to be part of life — to go out there every day and participate in the world, let alone try to experience it fully. It can feel so much easier to hide out; to be in the audience, watching the choices other people make; or to let someone else dictate our choices, then blame them for our lack of fulfillment.

My daughter has said, more than once, that memorizing lines is hard; for her, improv is a freeing alternative. Of course, she's 12. As we get older, and make more choices for ourselves, the stakes feel higher. What if we choose the wrong school, the wrong major, the wrong job, the wrong life?! As I hope this book has shown you, the answer to all those quandaries is to make another choice, and then another — and to realize that everyone else is out here doing the same thing. By building confidence in your ability to make choices for yourself, you learn that greater meaning, connection, fulfillment, and joy can always be just one choice away.

And, in that way, improvising adulthood is about cultivating an endless supply of hope.

I'll see you out there. I've got your back.

AFTERWORD

**"There is no real ending. It's just the
place where you stop the story."**

- Author Frank Herbert

*Last night, the stage was filled with improvisors creating something out of
nothing; in a few hours, it will be again. For now, it's empty. What stories
will next fill the space?*

I started this book by saying that I love my life, and I do. I love
my sweet, goofy, wise, creative, loving family. I love the sacred work
I do with my clients, helping them feel seen and heard, building up
their confidence around sharing their authentic voices with the world.
I love living in the Hudson Valley, where the benefits of being around
so many trees course through my nervous system every single day. I
love writing, and I loved writing this book.

Am I happy all day, every day? No, of course not. No one is. I still
face challenges. Sometimes I even have to relearn some of the lessons
I've shared with you here; I forget, and then I relearn.

But overall, I am so proud of the life I've created for myself.
And that is such a good feeling, one I want for all of you. Recently
Jordan and I took our daughter to Costa Rica, ready to share some
pura vida with her. We rented an Airbnb with a beautiful backyard,
complete with heliconias and a pool. One day, I was floating in the

water, delicate raindrops falling, and I was overcome with a full body feeling: *I paid for this experience with money I earned doing work I love that helps make other people's lives better.* A hummingbird flew by, and a yellow butterfly. Nearby, howler monkeys made their insane sounds, and I smiled. *Go on with your bad self.*

All those credentials I shared with you in the Introduction, they don't matter. What matters is that my life is an embodied commitment to following the "yes," and to saying "yes, and." When things start to feel out of alignment — when I start to feel a "no" — I know I will do something to shift myself closer to "yes."

I have my *own* back. And my deepest wish, for each of you, is that you have yours.

ACKNOWLEDGEMENTS

Thank you to my editors: Jordan, Dad, Mom, and Andy. You each gave me feedback that helped me elevate the quality of my storytelling and discover the true shape of the book I wanted to create. Thank you, too, to Kate, for reading an early draft and cheering me on.

Jordan, you read multiple drafts of this, while also growing your business and being an amazing dad and doing the three loads of laundry we seem to generate daily. You are always there for me, always, without fail. *Thank you.* I am so freaking lucky to have you as my partner in all things. To those of you who, like me, actually read the Acknowledgements section of books, you should go check out Jordan's music at jordanhirsch.net. The man can sing, something I discovered back in 1994 when he was Sky Masterson in Richard Montgomery High School's production of "Guys and Dolls." Swoon.

I also want to thank my daughter, Ali, for being such a source of inspiration. Ali, your you-ness inspires me to become an even fuller expression of myself. I hope this book is useful to you someday, and brings you comfort when you need it.

Thank you, too, to Washington Improv Theater in Washington, DC, and to all my teachers and friends from that community; without you, improv would never have become the force that it is in my life. You showed me what true connection and belonging feel like. Also, on *rare* occasion — very rare — you made me laugh.

Finally, thank you to everyone who has shaped the improv show that is my life, many but not all of whom are named in this book. It's an honor to share the stage with you.